DIPLOMAT

GUNNAR HAGGLOF
DIPLOMAT

MEMOIRS OF A SWEDISH ENVOY

IN LONDON · PARIS · BERLIN · MOSCOW

WASHINGTON

WITH A FOREWORD BY
GRAHAM GREENE

THE BODLEY HEAD
LONDON SYDNEY
TORONTO

ISBN 0 370 10274 6
Printed and bound in Great Britain for
The Bodley Head Ltd
9 Bow Street, London WC2E 7AL
by Richard Clay (The Chaucer Press), Ltd,
Bungay, Suffolk
Set in Monotype Ehrhardt
First published in English 1972

CONTENTS

Foreword vii

For Anna—of course

FOREWORD

Neutrality—there are few words which have been less understood by historians, politicians and the general public. To the general public in certain countries it is often a word spoken with a sense of moral superiority: among less fortunate countries, with equal unreason it is a word of reproach, as though there were a special virtue in being forced into an armed struggle. Gunnar Hagglof's memoirs make clear for the first time all that is required of those who direct neutrality, the interminable verbal war, the cunning employment of semantics, the perilous journeys from one warring country to another, the extreme prudence, the ability to judge between an empty and a real threat, the bluff which can be risked and the bluff which can be called—and behind all these manoeuvres a far from ignoble purpose, to save your country from the savagery of a world conflict and at the same time with extreme caution to do everything you can to aid the struggle against what you believe to be the evil side. In the last war Denmark lost a few lives in a token resistance and afterwards collaborated with the Germans hardly less than Vichy: it was Sweden—so often maligned—which saved the Western allies from the disastrous mistake of becoming involved in the Russian war against Finland; it was Sweden which at the height of German power refused to increase exports of war materials to Germany and kept her sea-lanes open across the Atlantic. Every country has what are called invisible exports and one of the most valuable invisible exports from Sweden to Great Britain in those war years was military intelligence.

It is no exaggeration to say that the young Hagglof, who had already been an *ancien ministre* at the age of 34, was the director of this whole perilous policy of what seemed in German eyes a very partial neutrality. It is an enthralling story: one day Gunnar Hagglof is in Washington trying unsuccessfully to purchase a heavy cruiser from the United States (a sad funny pilgrimage which began successfully enough with the President, continued by way of the Secretary of State, to the Chairman of the European Affairs

Committee, then on to Senator Vandenburg, to reach its bitter end with Senator Hiram Johnson whose opposition counted more than the President's support); another day he is linked in stubborn conference with Marshal Göring in Berlin ('You, Herr Hagglof, are an incorrigible lawyer and diplomat. You understand nothing of the great problems of the destiny of nations'); on another he arrives frozen at Leuchars from a plane to be offered by a kind official a tumbler of neat whisky to warm him. When he asked for a little water to dilute it, the official exclaimed with astonishment, 'But it's good whisky.'

And the result of all these dangerous and often abortive conferences? He has good reason to record it, though with no hint of personal pride, as he sits alone with a glass of Belgian beer on V.E. day at a little inn outside Waterloo (unwilling to be a neutral guest 'in the company of the people who had really fought against Hitler and his hordes'). He thinks of what a fragile construction neutrality had been: 'At the outbreak of the war twenty European states declared themselves neutral. Three of the neutrals were annexed to the Soviet Union—Estonia, Latvia and Lithuania. Eleven were attacked and most of them occupied—Denmark, Norway, the Netherlands, Belgium, Luxembourg, Finland, Romania, Hungary, Yugoslavia, Bulgaria and Greece. Only six of the twenty were spared to pursue their policy of neutrality—Sweden, Switzerland, Turkey, Spain, Portugal and Ireland.'

This is the exciting core of Gunnar Hagglof's memoirs, but there is great charm in the earlier pages when he is receiving a rare kind of diplomatic training—in France, Germany, Russia and England, under cultured and understanding ambassadors who left him leisure really to discover the countries to which he was posted. What other young foreign diplomat ever visited the depressed areas of England and Wales and lived in the homes of miners?

Eventually, after the war, as *doyen* for nine years of the Diplomatic Corps, he was forced (what a nightmare!) to attend 300 receptions a year. There must have been times when he looked back with nostalgia to the heroic days of the young 'neutral' diplomat who was as much in the front line saving lives as any fireman in the blitz.

[8]

'On my last night in Berlin the British bombers were very late in leaving. The whole of the Adlon was trembling under the impact of bombs falling in the vicinity. I left the shelter and stood for a minute in the monumental entrance hall, now abandoned by all staff. The heavy chandeliers were swinging. The front door had been blown open and I could see a great fire blazing on the opposite side of the Pariserplatz.

'I went out of the hotel and walked slowly down the Unter den Linden. The whole broad expanse of the avenue was illuminated by sky-high fires. The hot air blew clouds of dust and paper high above the burning buildings. In the middle of this Dante-esque valley of hell I discovered groups of dark figures. They were prisoners of war, sent out to clear the streets. They cheered the bombs. Round the equestrian statue of Frederick Wilhelm, French prisoners of war danced.

'This was my last night in Berlin.'

Graham Greene

PART ONE

I

Early Days

This is the story of a young man who became a diplomat without really wanting to. I suppose there are boys who at the age of ten have already made up their minds to become doctors or priests or even professional footballers. I was not one of them.

My mother loved music and played the piano almost as a virtuoso. At the same time she had a remarkable sense of order, an inheritance no doubt from generations of judges. Her father had been a Speaker of the Swedish parliament.

It was an expression of her sense of order that all her life she kept a diary. On the date of October 25, 1926, she noted, 'Gunnar has passed his final examination in law at Uppsala.' Six days later she made another entry: 'It is not yet decided if Gunnar will stay at home or will go abroad this winter.'

That same day my parents had discussed plans for my future with me. The following morning I went for a long walk on the beautiful island which lies off Stockholm as you sail in from the distant Baltic. This island is a vast park where one can easily walk for an hour or two.

I have never been much of a long-term planner for myself. That autumn, however, I was facing an urgent problem: should I go back to the University and continue my studies with a view to an academic career? Or should I go abroad and try to join an international organization? I had just passed my examination and I was only twenty-one.

In the Faculty of Law there were professors who had encouraged me to continue my studies with an academic career as my goal. Mr Unden, who was a professor of Civil Law although he now and then served as Foreign Minister, asked me if I wouldn't like to stay on at the University, and I felt honoured by his encouragement.

My father had always hoped that I would choose an academic career; although he was a banker, his five or six years at the University of Uppsala remained in his mind as the most wonderful period of his life. His only sister had married a descendant of Linnaeus, the great eighteenth-century botanist whom we in Sweden always call 'the king of flowers'. My Uncle Tycho was also a botanist, an ardent gardener and a poet. When I was a boy my father sent me to stay in Uncle Tycho's wonderful old manor house in Uppsala, full of eighteenth-century furniture and Linnaeus collections. The garden was designed by 'the king of flowers' himself. From my window on the upper floor I could see Uncle Tycho in the early morning, walking round the garden greeting his favourite flowers. He bowed so deeply—or even knelt—when speaking to them that he looked as if he was in prayer before them.

It was in this house that my father had lived when he was a young student. To him it seemed that there could be nothing more desirable than to live always in Uppsala.

But would I really like to stay for ever at the University? This was the question which I had to face.

I had nominally spent three years at the University of Uppsala, although my military service had shortened my actual studies to a little more than two.

It was a great relief, after a year and a half of military service, to lead a free academic life with friends and books. I belonged to a group of students and dons, and we had our meals in a house we rented together. This became my real home in Uppsala. We would spend hours after lunch or dinner talking and laughing. Often our discussions were continued in our lodgings well into the night.

Examinations were always celebrated by large drinking parties, ending up in the early morning with singing competitions or (even worse) all sorts of boisterous behaviour. A friend of mine succeeded once in pushing one of the old cannons which stood on the hill of the sixteenth-century Uppsala Castle right down to the main street —fortunately deserted in the middle of the night. Another friend, who was fond of riding, one night rode his favourite white horse upstairs to the second floor to wake up a student whom he had missed at the party.

The police were always very tolerant with us. We used to send them a box of cigars as a sort of apology after a particularly noisy night.

I found it not too difficult to pass an examination every second month. As there were thirteen such examinations in the juridical curriculum this would lead me to my final examination in roughly two years. I had plenty of time for other occupations. Uppsala is only forty minutes by train from Stockholm. It was easy to slip off and go to a dinner and dance and come back the following morning. There were other opportunities of a more serious nature. I went to listen to the then leading philosopher in Sweden, Mr Häger-ström, whose severe and deeply lined face greatly impressed me. He was not easy to understand. My almost exact contemporary, Dag Hammarskjöld, tried sometimes to explain the great philo-sopher's complicated theories and arguments to me. I can't say that Dag had a gift for making a problem any easier to understand; rather the reverse. However, we enjoyed these dialectic exercises as we walked from the University to the Castle, where Dag lived with his father, the Governor of Uppsala.

The older Hammarskjöld was a formidable personality. He had been Prime Minister during the First World War and he was a lawyer of international repute. He was also a conservative of the old school. As a young student I only had to bow to him; later in life I was to know him a little better.

Dag had certainly inherited much of his intellectual brilliance from his father's family, which for generations had produced out-standing lawyers, military commanders and ministers of the Crown. But his charm, his romanticism and the mysticism which emerged at a much later period of his life, came from his mother's family, of which the great genius of Swedish romantic literature, Johan Love Almquist, was a member.

The greatest event in a young Swede's life used to be his bacca-laureat when he was allowed to don the student's white cap. Dag was, of course, extremely successful at school and in his final paper he had obtained the highest possible marks in all but three or four subjects. He was eager to show his father the paper. It was certainly not to boast about his success—this was never in his character—but to give his father pleasure. The old governor put on his pince-nez and scrutinized the figures carefully. Silence. Then his father said: 'Your brother's were better.'

(The brother was Ake Hammarskjöld, in later life Secretary-General of the International Court of Justice in The Hague.)

When Dag told me the story, he laughed. But I felt that, sensitive as he was, he had suffered from his father's harshness.

But I am digressing in thinking of Dag, I said to myself as I was

[15]

walking on that October day in 1926. I sat down on a bench at the very end of the island, from which you can see all the sailing boats at anchor and the small white steamboats busily crossing from island to island in the wide archipelago outside Stockholm. But I saw little of all this while sitting there on that clear autumn day.

I had thought long enough about Uppsala; now I felt certain that I didn't want to spend the rest of my life there. The great dominating castle, the high—and badly restored—Gothic cathedral, the vast and often frozen plain stretching for miles round the town. No, I wouldn't be able to face this. My beloved Uncle Tycho had died at the age of almost eighty in 1920. He was infinitely closer to his ancestor Linnaeus of the eighteenth century than to the Uppsala of the 1920s.

This decision not to return to Uppsala gave me a feeling of great relief. Suddenly I remembered a morning in August 1925. My friend Thurn und Taxis, whom we all called Thurni, had set out with me from the little village of Les Plans, just below the Diablerets in Switzerland. It took us four hours to reach the Dent de Morcles through the passes round the Grand Muveran. Dent de Morcles is by no means one of the most famous mountains in the Swiss Alps, but it rises almost vertically from the valley of the Rhône, so one has a panoramic view of the whole gigantic world of the Alps.

Thurni and I climbed with the burning August sun on our backs. Three thousand feet below we saw the River Rhône as a dark blue line. It took us two hours to reach the summit. I was so exhausted that I fell headlong with my rucksack on my back. Thurni sat looking at the Alps, then he took his flute and played a gay tune from Vienna. We remained more than an hour on the summit of Dent de Morcles. Far to the west we saw in blinding sun the white-shrouded colossus of Mont Blanc. Ahead of us but on the other side of the valley of the Rhône we were confronted by the proud Dent du Midi. Farther away glittered some of the high summits of the Italian Alps.

'I was terribly frightened when we had to drag ourselves over that slippery block,' said Thurni suddenly.

'When I'm climbing I'm always frightened. That's the thrill, isn't it?' I replied. 'But I'm also admiring my own courage,' I added, laughing.

Then we sat for a while in silence. The splendour of the Alpine world was almost overwhelming.

'Listen, Gunnar,' Thurni said. 'What are you going to do when you've taken your degree?'

'Don't ask me,' I replied. 'I don't know myself. There's only one thing I'm certain of and that is that I would like to be a European.'

Thurni laughed and said that his family had always in a sense been European, as they had never been able to make up their minds to which country in central Europe they really belonged.

But when we returned to our pension in Les Plans Thurni told everybody that 'Gunnar will for ever be a European'. And for the rest of our mountaineering holiday I retained that name.

Now, sitting on my island bench near Stockholm, I felt rather embarrassed by my somewhat dramatic European declaration. I was brought up in a strict family discipline. One was not supposed to indulge in emotional eruptions. Emotions were reserved for such occasions as the concerts arranged by my mother when she collected a quartet or a quintet and we, the children, were allowed to listen from an upper floor in silence.

The school I went to had a partly military character. Quite a lot of our training was as future military men and in the First World War many of the most gifted boys in the upper classes decided to enter military service.

It was a period of rather demonstrative patriotic emotions. We marched to our shooting exercises with the feeling that we were going to fight the Russians, the 'hereditary enemies of Sweden' as the saying was. There was much talk of Charles XII, the king who for eighteen years waged war against Tsar Peter.

After the end of the First World War there came a reaction. My age group revolted against the military discipline of the school. We shocked our teachers by our new boldness. In the Literary Society, of which I was chairman for a year, we began to perform light French comedies, much to the disgust of the older teachers.

When we left school we were still in a mood of revolt. We turned against everything which could be called 'Oscarianism', the Swedish equivalent of 'Victorianism'.

In me, this produced a longing for foreign countries, because it

B

was during my visits to Germany, Switzerland and France that I had had the sensation of being free.

But is that really all I'm longing for, I asked myself, sitting on that bench? If so, then it is simply escapism. I knew there was something else. We who had been born before the First World War, and had been just old enough to realize the horror of it, felt a strong urge—a 'categorical imperative'—to find a new order in the world. In my fourteenth year I gave my mother as a Christmas present a book about President Wilson and an ode, written by me, to the future peace of the world.

When, slightly intoxicated by the grandeur of the Alpine world, I had proclaimed my wish 'to be a European' it had simply been an expression of my ambition to take some part in the building up of a new world order. At the University I had been one of the founders of a League of Nations association. I saw in the League the beginning of a new world and my real ambition was to work in the Secretariat of the League.

It was probably the atmosphere in the Faculty of Law at Uppsala which made me believe that the right way to get into the Secretariat was to study International Law, and I decided that what I should do was to write a thesis to become a doctor in that subject. The difficulty, however, was that I was only twenty-one, and one was not allowed to become a Doctor of Law before the age of twenty-five. I discussed all this with my father, and he undertook to pay for my studies at the Sorbonne in Paris for the next three or four years.

This decision meant that I should go to Paris in a few weeks' time to take up *sciences politiques*. It was a pleasant prospect, I thought, as I resumed my walk, now in the direction of Stockholm. I stopped for a cup of coffee at the old inn at the bridge across the canal. On the threshold I met Folke Arnander, a good friend of my eldest brother.* In his impulsive way Folke put his arm through mine and asked why I looked so pensive. When I explained, he said at once, 'But it's quite clear to me that you ought to go into the Diplomatic Service as an attaché. If you are sent to Paris, London, Berlin or the United States you will have time to read International Law at one

* Folke Arnander, secretary in the Swedish Diplomatic service; married in 1931 Lady Anne Lindsay, daughter of the Earl of Crawford and Balcarres.

of the universities. You won't need to stay long in the Diplomatic Service. You can quit as soon as you've got your doctor's degree'.

But, I replied, surely diplomats had to spend most of their time at parties, luncheons and dinners. I was very far from being a recluse, but I wouldn't like to become a figure in a perpetual pageant.

'Those are childish ideas,' Folke answered. 'Young diplomats have every chance to devote their free time to reading or to meeting people of their own choice. Look at me. I was an attaché in London for a long time and all my evenings were free. I didn't read much, but I met an endless number of interesting or amusing people. Some of them have become real friends.'

When I got home I wrote an application to the Ministry for Foreign Affairs to be examined for entry into the Diplomatic Service. I was about to send the letter when it suddenly occurred to me what a small chance there was that I would be accepted. I didn't know much about the nature of the examination, though I remembered vaguely that the previous year there had been eighteen or twenty applicants and only one had been admitted.

I hesitated for a moment at the letter-box. Then I told myself that I might as well try.

Thus it came about that, one November morning, I had to present myself at the Ministry of Foreign Affairs, an eighteenth-century palace just opposite the Royal Palace in Stockholm. I was in formal morning dress, as was the custom in those days.

The committee for the examination of applicants was composed of five or six men of considerable standing in Swedish public life. They conducted the examination entirely according to their own judgment. My first examiner was Baron Adelswärd, a big landowner who had been Minister of Finance and was now an elder statesman in the Liberal Party. I had met him at dinners with my parents and also at dances given for his daughters. It was about this that he spoke to me. We discussed the latest events in Stockholm society life. He spoke fluent French with a strong Swedish accent, which he took no trouble to correct. I have often wondered if this was the way French was spoken in the eighteenth century when the whole of the Swedish upper class spoke French in their everyday life.

Another examiner was a prominent Socialist Member of Parliament. He asked me, in French, to explain how Voltaire had defended

Calas. I wasn't at all sure of my facts so my answer was very hesitant. Luckily I was interrupted by my examiner, who recited from memory some of Voltaire's most brilliant diatribes. He then asked me if I had read *Candide*. As this masterpiece has always been one of my favourite books, I was able to give a fairly complete account.

On the whole I was very lucky. One examiner asked me to make a survey of the unification of Italy in the nineteenth century. Only a month earlier, I had read Paleologue's book on Cavour!

In the late afternoon I was informed that I was accepted and that I ought to report for service in the Ministry within the next few days.

At our family dinner that evening I mentioned that I had passed the examination for the Foreign Service. In my mother's diary for that day she wrote: 'Gunnar had his great examination for the Foreign Service and was accepted. We were astounded.' This was not surprising as my parents didn't know that I had applied for the examination.

What my mother did not write was that my father was rather unhappy about the news. He had little respect for the Swedish Diplomatic Service. He had himself been asked to join it in the 1880s, but had refused. 'Swedish diplomats only think of luncheons, dinners, rank and precedence, decorations and court uniforms,' he used to grumble. I assured him that I would not remain for long in this superficial diplomatic world.

A few days later I went to work in the Ministry for Foreign Affairs. I remember that the same night I was invited to a ball given by Professor Tengbom* and his wife. It was one of the gayest dances I have ever attended. At the traditional dances in Stockholm there were always the same young girls and the same young men dressed in uniform or in white-tie evening dress. At 10 p.m. supper was served and the dance went on to 1 a.m. In Professor Tengbom's house everything was different. Apart from dancing, there was always somebody playing on the lute, somebody singing, somebody organizing a charade. It was endless fun. The two daughters, Yvonne and Ann-Mari, were, of course, the centre of it all. Ann-Mari, who as a schoolgirl had danced with me at the Spring Ball in Uppsala, had not yet blossomed out in her full beauty but she always had endless charm, happy laughter and a zest for life.

* Professor Ivar Tengbom was one of Sweden's foremost architects. His daughter, Ann-Mari, married Prince Otto Bismarck.

There was much happiness and laughter in the 1920s. The Americans speak of 'the roaring twenties' and that expression might be fitting for their over-optimistic, over-expansionist decade.

In Germany as a young boy I had been overwhelmed by the turbulence of its cultural life. There was hardly any true happiness; it was mostly *angst* and tragic forebodings.

But as I remember the twenties in my own surroundings there was much happiness in the air. It was certainly not a dithyrambic happiness. On the contrary, there were undertones of a subtle irony, for many of us were deeply conscious of life's essential precariousness. Our existence was made gay by our youth and our hopes for the future, but there was a sadness also; hidden anxiety continually in our hearts.

I have never been a particularly 'literary' person, but when writing of the 1920s I cannot omit an experience which was for me unusual. While staying in Tours during the summer of 1926 I met a young man, who was, I think, a nephew of Justin Macarthy. He put into my hands a book of poetry by T. S. Eliot. This was my first experience of the 'new poetry'. Never will I forget my feelings when I first read the finale of *Prufrock*, which I have to quote even if it has now become a classical monument in English literature. I must have read it a hundred times and I am always carried away:

> *I have heard the mermaids singing, each to each.*
>
> *I do not think that they will sing to me.*
>
> *I have seen them riding seaward on the waves*
> *Combing the white hair of the waves blown back*
> *When the wind blows the water white and black.*
>
> *We have lingered in the chambers of the sea*
> *By sea-girls wreathed with seaweed red and brown*
> *Till human voices wake us, and we drown.*

For a long time I regarded this poem as the Mount Everest of poetry.*

---

* In the 1950s I came to know T. S. Eliot fairly well. One day I was bold enough to tell him that I thought the finale of *Prufrock* the finest poetry written in this century. He smiled his usual half-resigned, half-ironical smile and said, 'For a moment I thought the same, but only when I had just written it'.

From the middle of November I was working—if that is the word—in the Foreign Ministry. To be the youngest attaché was very pleasant in those days. The whole diplomatic staff was hardly more than thirty strong, and we all knew each other. It reminded me of 'our house' in Uppsala where old and young discussed freely together.

One of the sections in the Political Department was directed by Baron Eric Gyllenstierna of the same family as Shakespeare's Guildenstern. He had just inherited the family's vast entailed estate with its castle, Krapperup, in the south of Sweden just opposite Hamlet's castle, Kronborg, on the Danish side. The Secretary in the same section was a most charming man, Baron Louis de Geer, who spoke Swedish with a strong French accent and had also just inherited an important entailed estate, north of Stockholm. Sometimes when passing through the corridor of this section one could observe groups of serious-looking men dressed in black. They were the tenants from the estates who had come up to Stockholm to report to their masters.

In the 1920s, governments in Sweden changed almost every other year. When I entered the Foreign Service we had a Liberal Government and the Foreign Minister was Mr Löfgren, an international lawyer of some repute. He was a pleasant man, but very absent-minded. The first diplomatic luncheon I ever attended in my life was given in honour of the outgoing French Minister. Everybody arrived except the host, the Foreign Minister. We youngsters were sent out to find him, and find him we did. He was lunching by himself in the best restaurant in Stockholm.

Work went on at a leisurely pace. The older officials arrived towards eleven. An interval of two hours for luncheon was considered normal. At half past four we had tea. And at six we left our offices.

You might well ask: What did we do? My father, himself a busy banker and industrialist, often asked me this question.

In every Foreign Office there are certain sections which are self-explanatory. There must be a consular, a juridical, an administrative section and an archives department. All these are really auxiliaries to the central department, which concerns itself with policy.

What was Swedish foreign policy? The standard reply was that

Sweden's foreign policy was to have none. This always made my father laugh heartily.

But in reality this statement was nonsense. Every sovereign state must have a foreign policy if only because it is surrounded by other states and must concern itself with its own security.

It is not my intention to embark on a long essay on Sweden's foreign policy throughout the ages. But perhaps a few brief remarks may be of interest.

Sweden has sought security by building up a small empire round the Baltic. At the end of the seventeenth century Sweden-Finland was in control of the whole eastern shore, and also to a large extent the southern shore, of the Baltic. This vast sea had virtually become Swedish, with the exception of the coast of Denmark, Sweden's age-old rival.

But this Swedish Empire had been built up by Swedish arms over a long period when Russia was weak and Moscow seemed to belong to Asia rather than to Europe. But when Tsar Peter came to power in 1700 he soon set out to create a strong coalition against Sweden. For eighteen years young Charles XII of Sweden fought Russia, Poland, Prussia and Denmark, an almost unbelievable feat of arms. In the end Charles was killed in a campaign in Norway and the Swedish Empire fell like a house of cards. Only the heartland Sweden-Finland remained, with a few scattered possessions in northern Germany.

In the eighteenth century Sweden-Finland made two vain attempts to take revenge on Russia. During the Napoleonic period, Tsar Alexander I conquered Finland, which had been part of the Swedish kingdom for six hundred years. The year 1809 was one of the darkest in Swedish history. Finland was lost, Sweden was ruined, and an officers' revolt forced King Gustav IV to abdicate in favour of a childless old uncle.

The Swedish parliament elected a Danish prince to be Crown Prince of Sweden. He was careless enough to fall from his horse, breaking his neck.

The Government met to choose a new Crown Prince. They showed little imagination and opted for another Dane. But there have always been so many Danish princes.

Then, however, a curious incident occurred. The Ministers in Stockholm thought that it would be a clever move to have the approval of Napoleon, then at the height of his power. They wrote a dispatch to the Swedish Ambassador in Paris, asking him to submit their choice of the Danish prince to the Emperor. They hoped, of course, that Napoleon would ultimately help Sweden to reconquer their lost provinces from Russia.

The dispatch was sent by the ordinary diplomatic courier, who took two or three weeks to reach Paris. The Foreign Minister in Stockholm suddenly had the idea that, as the dispatch was so important, it would be prudent to send a copy by a second courier. As time was passing he sent a young cavalry officer, Count Mörner. This young man reached Paris long before the ordinary courier. Count Mörner apparently had a rather extravagant idea of the duties of a courier. He didn't deliver his letter to the Swedish Ambassador. Instead he went to pay his respects to Marshal Bernadotte, for whom he professed the greatest admiration. He explained to Bernadotte that the Swedish people needed a man like him to restore the former glories of Sweden.

The Marshal, who was on bad terms with Napoleon, was not slow to seize on the Count's suggestion, almost an offer. The young officer galloped back to Stockholm and told the Government that Marshal Bernadotte was available as a candidate. The Ministers' first thought was to put Mörner under arrest, but soon there was a wave of enthusiasm for the idea. So Bernadotte was elected Crown Prince of Sweden largely because the majority of the Swedish parliament hoped that the French Marshal would lead them to war, together with France, against Russia. But Bernadotte was more than a Marshal. He was a statesman.

He saw the impoverished state of Sweden. He realized the weakness of the Swedish armies. At the same time he was out of sympathy with Napoleon's imperial policies and his ambitions to establish a European hegemony.

Bernadotte decided to play a waiting game. He established contacts with Alexander of Russia. He gave the Tsar advice on how to handle Napoleon as an adversary. Alexander should avoid battles, withdraw, and force Napoleon to lengthen his supply-lines.

It was an extraordinary feat of diplomatic, military and parliamentary manoeuvring to bring the Swedish people, who really wanted a French victory over Russia, to enter the coalition against

Napoleon. Swedish troops fought in the battle of Leipzig, where Napoleon was decisively defeated.

Bernadotte's aim was to compensate for the loss of Finland by creating a union between Sweden and Norway, with himself as king, and he succeeded in this.

He didn't want this new double-monarchy to be involved in European power politics, as he saw that the two countries formed a unit relatively easy to defend. To make it even easier, he always tried to maintain friendly personal relations with the Russian Tsar. At the same time he realized that the security of the two Scandinavian countries must have as its background a balance of power between Russia on the one hand and Great Britain on the other. While he cultivated good relations with St Petersburg, he was happy to see the British Fleet cruising in the Baltic.

In this way the Swedish policy of non-alliance was born—the policy which later developed into one of neutrality. The begetter of Swedish neutrality was not the Swedish people, not even a born Swede, but a French Marshal.

This policy was pursued by Bernadotte, now Charles XIV, in a very pragmatic way. In the later half of the nineteenth century the Swedish Government and the Swedish people became more and more attached to this policy of neutrality. At the same time many Swedes were always haunted by their old fear of Russia. King Oscar II (1872–1907) believed that Russia was obsessed by a desire to obtain access to the Atlantic, and that therefore northern Scandinavia was a target for Russian expansionism. He felt the need for a counterweight and thought he could find it in the new imperial Germany, with which there were many ties of family and education.

The Court, the officers of the Army and the Navy and a considerable part of the upper and middle classes were in sympathy with the German-orientated royal attitude. The Liberal Party and the now emerging Social-Democratic Party on the other hand opposed and criticized the pro-German tendencies. To them a policy of strict neutrality was the best defence against dangerous trends in Swedish foreign policy.

When the First World War became, after the first few months, a relatively static war, this was to the advantage of the neutrals. In fact all the northern neutrals, with the tragic exception of Belgium, succeeded in remaining on the outside. The Netherlands, Denmark,

Norway and Sweden found that neutrality had stood the test of time and their peoples became more than ever attached to this now traditional policy.

The outcome of the war brought the northern neutrals great advantages. Previously, Sweden's foreign policy had consisted mainly of anxiously watching its two formidable neighbours, the Tsar's Russia and the Kaiser's Germany. When both had fallen to the ground Sweden could look across the Baltic at a chain of small, independent states, some of which were attached to Sweden by long historical traditions. Thus Sweden had every reason to greet the new Europe with satisfaction, and Swedish foreign policy could concentrate on the task of strengthening the new League of Nations.

It was, in fact, the problems of the League which were the centre of discussion in the Ministry of Foreign Affairs when I arrived there. One day when the Under-Secretary for Political Affairs saw me in vigorous discussion with some older officials he said with a smile, 'Jesus preaching in the Temple at the age of twelve.' This *mot* found its way round the Ministry and must have reached the ear of the Foreign Minister.

As the youngest attaché I was often on duty in the evenings and on Sundays. One Sunday morning when I was sitting in the cipher room the hall porter came to inform me that the Japanese Minister had arrived with his staff, asking to be received immediately by the Foreign Minister or his representative. They seemed to be in a very agitated state, the hall porter added.

I made some attempts to reach the Foreign Minister or any of the higher officials, but without success, so I decided to receive the Japanese gentlemen myself. I told the hall porter to conduct them to the Foreign Minister's waiting room, and in this very impressive room I received them. To an accompaniment of great lamentations by his assistants, the Japanese Minister read an announcement that the Emperor of Japan had died. I expressed the Swedish Government's condolences in a short speech, which was drowned by the loud and strange expressions of sorrow by the Japanese.

This story must have amused the Foreign Minister, for he remarked to the Permanent Secretary, 'Now Jesus also receives in the temple.'

After little more than two months in the Ministry I was ordered to the Legation in Paris. Nothing could have pleased me more. The night before my departure I went with my mother to the opera. It was *The Meistersingers*, and when I heard Walther's spring song I experienced such an intense flood of happiness that I could not restrain my tears. I was young, I was free, and I was going to Paris.

II
Paris

At the age of twenty-one I had probably travelled more widely than most of my Swedish friends, but, of course, my mileage would not be so great by the standards of today. In the 1920s travelling was still a sort of discovery. Nowadays the young have, in a sense, seen almost everything in advance; there are so many films and travel books with perfectly coloured photographs. In our geography books in the twenties we had only a few rather faint illustrations. And the youth of today fly around the world. Recently I met a young man who had just been from Europe to Japan and back on a quite inexpensive student's ticket. The radius of his travelling is already wider than mine, though I have been travelling constantly over a period of fifty years.

However, at twenty-one, I seemed then to have covered quite a lot of ground. I had spent a summer in northern Germany, another summer in Berlin, four months in Switzerland and three in Tours. When my father celebrated his sixtieth birthday he took the family—a whole railway carriage—to Rome for a month. This was a journey which had been prepared for by many months of reading, a journey which became a great event in my life.

Had I then been asked to make a list of the cities of the world it was most essential to see, I would undoubtedly have put Rome at the top of the list. Although Berlin was the great city which I knew best in my youth, I would hardly have listed it as essential. In my eyes Berlin was something intensely stimulating, almost startling, but not a 'must'.

Certainly I would have listed Paris as a good second after Rome. During my years of studying history I had built up a picture of France, particularly the France of the great seventeenth century. And even the most inexperienced apprentice in the diplomatic profession was bound to realize that Paris in the 1920s was the very centre of the world's diplomacy.

As a youthful enthusiast of Europe I saw Paris as the natural capital of future European unity. I liked to stand at the great obelisk in the Place de la Concorde, surveying that incomparable scene, my eyes making the wide arc from the colonnades of the Chamber of Deputies, the Tuileries gardens with the Louvre in the background, the magnificent façades of the Ministry of Marine and the Hotel Crillon, to the unique vista of the Champs-Élysées, culminating in the distance in the crowning Arc de Triomphe. Was this not the natural capital of Europe?

I had plenty of time to discover Paris. I reported to the Swedish Legation and was presented to my new chief, Count Ehrensvärd. This elderly gentleman received me in a rather absent-minded way. He talked for a while about the policies of the League of Nations, then concluded by saying that he had no instructions to give me except that he didn't want to see me in the Chancery after luncheon. 'There are so many better things to do in Paris than to sit and scribble in an office.'

This meant that I was free in the afternoons, the evenings and the nights to go discovering Paris. At that time one was still able to stroll the streets of Paris, pass an hour or two with the *bouquinistes* on the quays of the Seine, wander through the Middle Ages and the Great Century to the Luxembourg gardens, drop in at a lecture at the Sorbonne and then sit in a café talking with French friends while the gas-lamps lit up along the darkening boulevards. In the 1920s man was still master of his city.

I suppose everyone who has had the good fortune to spend a year of his youth in Paris retains in his memory a picture somewhat embellished in the course of later years. When I poured out my enthusiasm for Paris there were always some elderly gentlemen who remarked with a slightly superior smile: 'Ah, but you should have seen Paris before 1914. Then it was *really* wonderful.' There have probably always been elderly gentlemen speaking in nostalgic tones of the 'really wonderful' Paris *they* knew in *their* youth. So one could go back from one generation to another and say, with Talleyrand, that unless one had known the years before 1789 one would never understand the pleasure and happiness which life can offer (*'ne sait pas que c'est le plaisir de vivre'*).

The Paris I like to remember is the Paris of the late 1920s. The turbulence of the first post-war years had somewhat abated. But the pace of life was still rather high. Conversation was fast and lively;

an apt paradox now and then was appreciated in the salon of the Duchess de la Rochefoucauld.

I remember sitting as one of a semicircle round the armchair of Paul Valéry. '*Le mâitre désire son chocolat*,' the Duchess whispered to her butler. In a moment Valéry was in full swing, analysing a book which had just been published, a scientific problem which he was on the point of solving or a political event which had made the headlines in the morning's newspapers. His conversation was so superior that, probably against his own wishes, it often became one long monologue. André Maurois used to sit at the feet of Valéry, putting in, every now and then, a *bon mot*. I sat in strict silence near the door.

But I was not the only silent listener. André Tardieu, later several times Prime Minister and a man of great self-confidence, sat for more than an hour listening to '*le Maître*' without saying a word. It was not simply the brilliance of Valéry's talk that kept one silenced. Not only did he love a paradoxical expression but also a paradoxical process of thought. He would toy with alternative lines of reasoning; who would want to distract him with a remark when he had just reversed his arguments and begun to contradict what he had proved a moment ago with such blinding Cartesian logic?

Of course, Valéry was brilliant, yet I could never really appreciate his books. My taste was less intellectual. During my first weeks in Paris I read with intense interest the two novels by Raymond Radiguet, *Le Diable au Corps* and *Le Bal du Comte d'Orgel*. In the early summer of 1927 I began to read Marcel Proust. It became an enchantment to see the world and oneself in an entirely new way: as '*une vision douteuse et à chaque minute anéantié par l'oubli, la réalité précedénte s'évanouissant devant celle qui lui succède, comme une projection de lanterne magique devant la suivante quand on a changé le verre*'. I read Proust with the greatest intensity for two months. The dose was probably too strong. My passion turned into something almost like an aversion, to which Proust's excessive social snobbism and the artificiality of the whole world of his novel certainly contributed.

It was Stendhal, the opposite of Proust, who now attracted me. In the autumn of 1927, I read *La Chartreuse de Parme* for the first time. I was ill in bed and my French nurse read aloud to me. My chief, Count Ehrensvärd, came to visit me. He was delighted when he found us reading Stendhal. He immediately began to discuss various chapters in the book. When I said that I hadn't got that far in my reading he looked at me with an expression of the greatest surprise. 'Do you really mean that you haven't read *La Chartreuse* before?' I admitted this lack of education, and he remained silent for a while. Then he said, 'To be young, to live in Paris and to read for the first time *La Chartreuse de Parme*—what more can one ask of life?'

Ehrensvärd was a man of great culture. By birth an aristocrat from the south of Sweden, he had become a Liberal by deep personal conviction. He had been Foreign Minister in one of the Liberal Governments before the war.

In Sweden the political struggle between Conservatives and Liberals had assumed a bitter and at times a very violent character—not unlike the situation in Great Britain at the same period. Ehrensvärd was regarded by many Conservatives as a traitor to his class. His elder brother was a close friend of King Gustaf and a staunch Conservative. When the two brothers happened to be at the family's castle at the same time the park had to be divided into two parts so that the brothers could take their morning constitutional without risk of meeting each other.

To my chief, France was more than a second homeland. He had a true passion for French literature, painting, sculpture and architecture, indeed the whole French way of life. He devoted the greatest part of his working time to writing essays on French poetry and translating French masterpieces into Swedish.

He had little or no interest in economic or commercial matters. After listening to a report on the necessity for a new trade agreement with France, he remarked in a rather reproachful way, 'But, my dear Counsellor, why should governments interfere with commerce? That is the business of the merchants'.

He came to the Chancery quite early in the morning. When he had read the leading articles in *Le Temps* and *Le Journal des Debats*, he rang for his Counsellor or his attaché to assist him when he opened the official correspondence. This was a rather strange procedure. He opened the letters in order to see which of them was signed by the Foreign Minister. Those which were, he placed carefully together on his desk. But the rest he dropped on the floor, and it was the assistant's duty to read them and report to him if any was important enough for him to read.

When this business was happily completed, Ehrensvärd began his morning conversation. To me he usually talked about a book he had been reading or some painting he had seen the previous day. He had a remarkable memory. One morning he spoke of a French governmental crisis at the beginning of the twentieth century. When I showed my surprise that he could remember all these details, he said that he had followed the political events in the Third Republic since he was at school. I mentioned that I was studying a book in which I had found a list of all French governments since 1871. Ehrensvärd asked me to bring the book, so that I should be able to check him when he enumerated all these governments. He succeeded almost one hundred per cent in this almost incredible feat of memory. He missed only two governments, both of which had lasted only some three or four days.

Ehrensvärd had the generous but sometimes puzzling habit of assuming that one had the same massive knowledge as himself. One morning he said, 'You remember, of course, the apse of the cathedral in Amiens.' When I had to confess my ignorance he gave me an absolutely brilliant exposé of the history of Gothic architecture, against a background of the cathedral in Amiens, which he found the most admirable. Another day he started his morning conversation by saying, 'You must remember the poem Voltaire dedicated to Louisa Ulrika' (later Queen of Sweden). When I said I did not, he recited from memory this poem in French, and added his own translation into Swedish. He then gave me one of his books on French classical literature with one verse of Voltaire's poem as a dedication:

S'occuper, c'est savoir jouir
L'oisiveté pèse et tourmente
L'âme est un feu qu'il faut nourrir
et qui s'éteint s'il ne s'augmente.

The paths which Ehrensvärd followed in his wanderings through French literature could be marked: from Rabelais to Montaigne, from Malherbe to Boileau and from La Fontaine to Voltaire. But he left aside Pascal and Racine, not to speak of Bossuet or Claudel.

I had read far too much of Sainte-Beuve's *Port Royal* not to miss the religious element in Ehrensvärd's picture of French literature. Have there not been in French culture during the last four or five centuries two contrasting and therefore particularly fertile currents of inspiration marked by the names of Pascal, Racine and Claudel on one side and of Montaigne, Voltaire and Valéry on the other?

I found it more rewarding to listen to Count Ehrensvärd's monologues on political problems. He was worried about the political structure of Europe after the First World War. Contrary to the general opinion in Sweden, he found the Treaty of Versailles too mild. The formidable state which Bismarck had created had remained almost intact, while Britain and the United States had left France without any military guarantees. The French frontier between France and Germany should have been fixed at the Rhine, giving the French the opportunity of building fortifications along the left bank.

He thought the Swedish Government put too much trust in the League of Nations. In the final analysis, the whole European order was dependent on Britain's willingness to give its support to France at an early stage of any critical situation. 'It was only at the very last moment that Britain came forward in 1914,' he said. 'It won't be easier next time, now that the British have lost millions of their best men.'

I was an enthusiast for the League of Nations, for the Treaty of Locarno and for Briand's policy of appeasement between France and Germany. Ehrensvärd's answer was that the value of the Locarno Treaty depended entirely on Britain's readiness to fulfil its guarantee. The Italian guarantee was of little or no real value. As to the policy of Briand, it had perhaps led to a better atmosphere, but not to any tangible results. When I spoke about Briand's and Stresemann's famous meeting in Thoiry, Ehrensvärd retorted, 'Don't talk so much about Thoiry. It was a luncheon, not a treaty'.

Once every week Countess Ehrensvärd was 'at home' and received whoever felt entitled to present himself at the Minister's residence in the Avenue Marceau. It was my duty to be present at these weekly receptions, for whenever the Countess didn't recognize a visitor she made a sign to me and then it was my job to greet the newcomers and find out their identity. This amused me a great deal and was, in fact, excellent training for a diplomatic apprentice.

In the 1920s Paris and London together made up the world's

most important diplomatic centre, though I don't think the total number of foreign diplomats in Paris was more than about three hundred—a small percentage of the diplomatic mass formations of the present day. Of these three hundred, only some thirty or forty were seen in French society. Many were probably too busy in their chanceries. A British third secretary, D. W. Lascelles, told me he detested being stationed in Paris as he often had to spend ten hours a day ciphering and deciphering telegrams. As we walked through rue du Faubourg-Saint Honoré and came to the entrance to the British Embassy, he said, 'I wish they would transfer me to Addis Ababa. They had only ten cipher telegrams last year'.

There were only eleven ambassadors in Paris in those days. The most monumental was the British Ambassador, Lord Crewe, a Liberal elder statesman and *grand seigneur*. It made a wonderful picture to see this tall, distinguished elderly gentleman receiving his guests in his elegant embassy, which had been built for Pauline Bonaparte, but ever since the days of the Duke of Wellington had been the British Embassy. The Marquess of Crewe stood alone most of the time when receiving guests at his receptions. His wife, a daughter of the former Prime Minister, Lord Rosebery, could not bear to shake hands for more than twenty minutes.

Twenty years later I reminded the delightful and witty Lady Crewe of those receptions. She laughed and said, 'Your description is perfectly right. I have always found big receptions the most meaningless form of society life.' My wife often reminded me of Lady Crewe's words when, for nine years of my life, it was my duty as doyen of the Diplomatic Corps in London to attend three hundred receptions a year.

A young attaché in the 1920s enjoyed infinitely more freedom. Paris offered such a variety of attractions. There were the elegant dances given by the Clermont Tonnères or the de Broglies. There were the innumerable dances for debutantes, where a second or third dance with the same girl would provoke whisperings among the mothers or chaperones sitting round the ballroom. There was the international set, which included many foreign royalties. I remember a ball where I was stunned by the extraordinary beauty of Princess Marina of Greece, later the Duchess of Kent.

Outside the boundaries of high society there were other attractions. I sat one night dining with a friend in a restaurant in Montmartre. At the end of a good meal I remarked that we really ought to do something for the people in the street, who perhaps had had no dinner. My friend, who was a rather wealthy young man, and I walked along the Boulevard de Clichy. In one of the small side streets we found a café where we succeeded in persuading the *patron* to let us have his place for the evening. We opened the doors and offered free drinks. The news spread like wildfire around the quarter. Soon we had to limit the number of guests. We did this by laying down the rule that everybody claiming a drink should give a performance of some sort. Some responded with a song, others with acrobatics. After an hour or so there were some sixty or seventy people singing in and outside our café. Then, of course, the police intervened. Two gendarmes closed the doors and led us away to the nearest police station. We made a full and frank confession and were given a Caporal cigarette, with the friendly advice to go home and sleep.

One evening in May 1927 I was invited to a ball in a house near the Place des Vosges. It was a wonderful night and we danced until early morning. When I drove back through the rue de Rivoli and the Champs-Élysées I found groups of people cheering in the streets. I stopped my car to enquire. 'Lindbergh has done it,' was the answer. I had, of course, read about the young airman with the Swedish name, but I had no idea that he was expected in Paris that night. Expected he was, because my informants in the street told me that there had been tens of thousands to meet him on the airfield.

Early the following morning I was asked to see my chief. Count Ehrensvärd had a number of telegrams before him. 'It seems,' he said to me, 'that there is a young man by the name of Lindbergh who has flown across the Atlantic. In Stockholm they are very excited about this feat by somebody they would like to consider as a Swedish American. They want me to arrange some manifestation here in Paris. I am not sure that the French or the Americans will like us to, as it's obviously meant to be a great American–French gesture, but will you go down to the American Embassy and speak to Mr Lindbergh?'

I found the streets around the American Embassy packed with people. I had first to telephone a friend among the American secretaries, then, with the help of about ten French policemen, I was at last safely ushered into the residence of the American Ambassador, Mr Myron T. Herrick. Six or seven people were waiting in a drawing-room. I was told that Lindbergh was still asleep. As he had been flying alone for thirty-three hours, one could well understand that he needed some rest.

We waited, and an hour or two later the door opened and in came Lindbergh. With a smile he excused himself for not having had time to dress properly. He was wearing a dressing-gown, probably the Ambassador's, as it was much too short for Lindbergh. The tall young man stood upright in the centre of the drawing-room, obviously very shy, but also very happy. Then he went round and spoke to each one of us. When I mentioned the intense enthusiasm in Sweden, he smiled and said: 'Yes, I know. My grandfather came from there. He was Swedish, but I am American.'

I tried to explain that the Swedish Minister and the Swedish community in Paris would like to organize a celebration in his honour. Lindbergh answered, 'You know, my idea was to see Paris by myself. But there were so many people waiting to meet me I'm afraid I will have a heavy programme. But, of course, if there is time I would like to meet the Swedes'.

A Frenchman interrupted to ask Lindbergh if it was true that he had had only a small pocket compass to guide him during his flight. At once Lindbergh's manner changed. 'How can people believe such nonsense,' he exclaimed almost angrily. 'I am an experienced pilot. I have checked and rechecked my compass and I can assure you that it is a very reliable instrument.'

I was happy to have seen for a fleeting moment the real Lindbergh, the man, who by his own will-power, hard work and extraordinary courage, had conquered the Atlantic alone.

There was always something new happening in a young attaché's life.

In April 1927 the King of Sweden came on a visit to Paris. King Gustaf V was a very tall man with the manners of a real *grand seigneur*. Every spring he spent some months in France, mostly on the Riviera, to see his numerous friends and to play tennis. This time he had to leave Paris fairly soon in order to pay a state visit to King Alfonso of Spain. I was ordered to go in advance to Madrid to take part in the preparations. On the day of the King's arrival there was a great assembly of dignitaries at the railway station. The Papal Nuncio in his cardinal's robes stood at the head of the Diplomatic Corps. At last King Alfonso appeared, wearing a Prussian-looking uniform and a silver helmet crowned by an eagle, a rather absurd outfit, but he carried it off with his usual elegance and nonchalance. When he greeted the Nuncio he lifted the prelate's hand, with the episcopal ring, towards his lips, but at the last moment the Nuncio withdrew his hand. This ceremony had been observed for several centuries whenever the Spanish monarch greeted the representative of the Pope.

Then the train arrived and King Alfonso presented the Spanish dignitaries to his royal Swedish guest. There I saw for the first time the Prime Minister, Primo de Rivera, a rather fat general looking more like a friendly, elderly uncle than a dictator. King Alfonso spoke to him as to everybody else in an easy, rather informal way, now and then whispering something amusing in the ear of his guest. It was obvious that the two Kings enjoyed each other's company.

We left the station in a long procession of cars. I sat in the last car, at the side of an elderly Spanish gentleman. Crowds lined the streets, and it struck me that they were all men dressed in black and all raised their bowler hats stiffly at regular intervals as the cars went by. When I drew the attention of my neighbour to this he laughed at my simplicity. 'They are policemen, all of them,' he said. 'It is, of course, not because of the King of Sweden that we take such precautions. But there have been so many attempts on King Alfonso's life.'

In the evening a splendid banquet was given in the royal palace. My modest title of attaché had erroneously been translated into *Agregado Militar*, which gave me a far too high-ranking place at the dinner table. I sat between the Duquesa de la Vitoria and a Condesa de los Andes, which I found very grand.

But what impressed me that first evening—and what I found in the course of the whole visit typical of the Spanish Court and the circle round King Alfonso—was the easy-going and light-hearted style of conversation. For instance, the Spanish grandees didn't address the King as 'your Majesty'. They said simply, 'Don Alfonso'.

[37]

After the dinner we were all gathered in a long gallery while King Gustaf went round bestowing decorations upon a number of Spanish dignitaries. I was standing in another part of the gallery in lively conversation with some Spanish gentlemen when somebody tapped me on the shoulder. I turned and there was King Alfonso, followed as always by the Duke of Miranda. 'Look, Miranda,' the King said. 'Here is a young man who has never been decorated before. What happiness to be so young.' Turning to me he said, 'I really envy you your youth and even more your freedom. To be born a King is really a hard fate. Everybody has claims on me. But my most cruel tyrant is, of course, Miranda. Look at him! Even here in my palace he carries his stick'. As Marshal of the Court, Miranda held a white ivory baton, the top of which was in the form of a hand.

Spanish officials formed a circle round us while the King affixed to my uniform the insignia of a Knight of the Order of Isabella Catholica. 'My young friend,' he said, 'you will certainly receive many decorations in the future. But promise me always to wear the order which I now bestow on you, and remember the unhappy Don Alfonso who always had to live under the stick of the cruel Miranda.'

'Let me tell you what happened last summer. I went on my annual holiday to Deauville. The first evening I felt so free and happy that I went to the Casino to play *chemin de fer*. I sat up very late and I had just gone to bed in my hotel when Miranda came into my room to remind me that I had to go to morning Mass. I am accustomed to this. But what is so awkward in the church in Deauville is that they always seat me in a big armchair right under the pulpit. Miranda was seated far behind and was quite unable to keep me awake. It seems that the priest gave a very long sermon. He ended up by calling for a collection to build a new church and in a loud voice he announced, "What is needed is 500,000 francs." This woke me and I shouted "Banco!"'

Our whole group, including the King and Miranda, burst into laughter. The King went on: 'You can imagine how Miranda looked at me when we were back in the hotel. He said very sternly that I had better keep to my rooms while he would try to prevent the story from reaching the newspapers. So there I sat, all alone, reflecting gloomily on my life. In the afternoon, fortunately, I received telegrams about troubles in Madrid so I jumped into my Bugatti and returned home at top speed.'

In the following days King Alfonso showed his royal guest round Madrid and Toledo. He always had new and amusing stories to tell. But when we came to the Escorial he stood for a moment in silence contemplating the royal tombs. Then he said: 'Yes. Here they are buried, all my ancestors. There is only one place left—over there in that corner—and that is where I shall be buried.'

After ten days in Spain I reported back to Paris. Count Ehrensvärd listened to my descriptions of the Spanish countryside. When I extolled the grandeur of the Castilian landscape, Ehrensvärd retorted, 'I prefer France and Italy. They are countries *mieux meublés* than Spain'.

He said that during my absence he had been thinking about my position. He wished me to stay in Paris for some years. It was not enough to stay only one year if one wanted to grasp the essentials of French civilization. I was delighted to hear him saying this because I had begun to be more and more attracted by the French language and by my friends in Paris.

Little did I realize that the curse of diplomatic life is—and will presumably always remain—the habit Ministries of Foreign Affairs have of transferring their representatives abroad to another post exactly when they are beginning to understand the countries where they are stationed.

After hardly one year in Paris I was ordered to leave. The Ministry in Stockholm let me know that they found that I had devoted too much of my time in Paris to dinners, dances, parties and social life in general. The time had come for me to see the tougher sides of life. To that end I was transferred to the Consulate-General in London.

III

London

This was my first visit to England. But to tell the truth it was not so much England as the farewell to France which occupied my mind as I left the French coastline behind me at Calais.

To console myself I read Voltaire's *Candide*, sitting on the ferry-boat on a sunny day in February 1928. When I finished reading this masterpiece and looked up I saw for the first time in my life the white cliffs of Dover. I was twenty-three.

As most Scandinavians do, I thought we were so like the English that it would be easy to understand England and to make English friends.

Nobody met me at Victoria. A taxi drove me through a grey fog to a sombre hotel in Great Portland Street. It was cold and damp in my room. I struggled for half an hour with the gas stove before I understood that I should put a shilling in the meter. I thought with longing of Paris. Had anybody whispered in my ear that I was destined to spend more than twenty years of my life in London I would have been cast into the deepest gloom.

Next morning, walking towards the Consulate in High Holborn, I felt bewildered. I was used to great cities like Berlin or Paris, cities built to a geometrical design—circles, squares or straight lines. Making my way along High Holborn I found that the street was sometimes narrow, sometimes broad, and that the houses on one stretch were low-built, perhaps sixteenth century, on another stretch tall, modern office buildings; and on yet another a brick-red palace in the Gothic style of the nineteenth century.

When I entered the Consulate and asked to see the Consul-General the hall porter told me that he had no fixed hours for his work in the office. If I had some urgent business I should see the Vice-Consul when he was free.

I sat there waiting and pondering on this peculiar English atmo-sphere, a sort of absent-minded nonchalance. When I was admitted to the Vice-Consul, Mr Zenon Westrup, whom I had met in the house of Count Ehrensvärd in Paris, he knocked the ash out of his pipe and said, 'Oh, there you are'. We chatted for ten minutes, and it was decided that I should work in the general consular department, dealing with passports, shipping documents and the like.

I found this both amusing and strenuous. One met an incessant stream of people—sailors who wanted to change ships, tourists who had lost their passports or their money, damsels in distress, inventors offering new and revolutionary weapons to the Swedish Army, and many others. At 6 p.m. we closed the office and went to a pub on the other side of High Holborn to round off our working day with a pint of beer.

All this was pleasant, but the most important thing to me was to meet English people. Two of the secretaries in the British Embassy in Paris had given me letters of introduction to men in the Foreign Office. Folke Arnander had written to some of his numerous friends in or outside London. After a month or two I knew quite a few people, who introduced me to their clubs, invited me for weekends in the country and took me along to the races or to dances.

About three months after my arrival I wrote to my father, who had asked for my impressions of the English. After explaining my belief that we Swedes were so like the English that it would all be easy, I wrote:

This I have found to be a complete error. The English are very different from us, and in a rather complicated way. How can I illustrate this? You know that I like discussion. In Sweden, as in Germany, we try to develop our arguments in logical order. We take our turn to express our opinions. We like to try to reach some conclusions acceptable to all.

But this is not at all how people behave at a discussion in a club in London. I go often to a club called the Travellers'. There we are usually five or six, having tea and a chat. I say we 'chat' because nobody would accept such a pompous word as 'discuss'. Nobody is inclined to develop a real series of arguments. Everybody seems to assume that the others already know all possible arguments. One makes short remarks preferably with an amusing turn of phrase.

The conversation is rapid. Hints and allusions are enough. It would be considered pedantic to develop a lengthy argument. The unforgivable sin is to give an *exposé* which could be stamped as a

[41]

monologue. Then one is considered to be a bore and will be left alone in the smoking-room.

In Paris I listened to many brilliant conversations. There, of course, people often compete with more or less brilliant ideas. But in a London club it is not considered good taste to develop brilliant ideas.

It is often said that the English are very tied up with their traditions. Yes, this might be true when it comes to external pomp and ceremonies. But their attitude to history is far more complicated. When I lived in France, I was much impressed by the fact that the French are enormously conscious of their history. It is not only Verdun and Waterloo which live in the daily consciousness of the French; it is also Agincourt and Crécy. All this mass of remembered history is arranged in neatly defined layers. Every moderately well-educated Frenchman knows what belongs to the Middle Ages, to the Renaissance, the Great Century, the eighteenth century, the Revolution, the Napoleonic period, the Restoration, Louis Philippe, Napoleon III and the Third Republic.

Not so the English. They are far less burdened by their history. It might be thought that this is easy to explain because most Englishmen seem to think that England today is greater and more powerful than ever before. But I don't think that this is the right explanation. The English live in their history in a different way from the French. Their country has never been devastated by war and revolution as has been the case in France. This is perhaps the reason why they are so much at home in their own history. When they go to church on Sundays they are surrounded by monuments from the Middle Ages, but also monuments of the present day, as well as from the Renaissance and the seventeenth century. In England all past centuries are alive together with the present. In France people would be shocked if an eighteenth-century mansion was enlarged by a wing in modern style. In England they have never hesitated to mix styles. It is typical that such a particular style as the Gothic has never ceased to grow new shoots. Apart from the magnificent Gothic of the Middle Ages, England had a Gothic style in the eighteenth century and a well-developed Gothic in the nineteenth century—every morning I pass the Prudential Insurance company's main office in High Holborn, a Gothic creation from the late nineteenth century.

[42]

These impressions of a young foreigner in England, written more than forty years ago, may perhaps stand a little more quoting:

When I had luncheon yesterday with an English friend, I saw two gentlemen come into the dining-room somewhat later than the other members. One was the Prime Minister, Stanley Baldwin, and the other was Lord Balfour. I whispered to my friend to draw his attention to the two illustrious gentlemen. But he didn't even turn his head. He simply said, 'The Prime Minister comes every now and then'. I looked round the dining-room. Nobody was paying the slightest attention to the two statesmen, although I am convinced that everybody was well aware of their presence.

Imagine what would happen if Messieurs Clemenceau and Poincaré were to enter the dining-room in the Circle Interallié in Paris! How many surprised, enthusiastic or critical exclamations! The conversation at all the luncheon tables would immediately rise to a crescendo!

It could, of course, be said that the little scene in the dining-room of the Travellers' is nothing but another example of the Englishmen's well-known phlegm. But how is it now with this famous phlegm?

As often as I can I spend an hour or two in the House of Commons. There is little sign of phlegm there. I have never seen an assembly where the atmosphere changes so rapidly. In a moment the mood of the House can change from hilarious laughter to thundering indignation. The House of Commons is the best dramatic theatre in London.

What vexed me was my English friends' complete lack of interest in Sweden. I wrote home:

You cannot imagine how little the English know of Sweden. I readily admit that our information service is bad. But I am convinced that even if we were the ablest propagandists Sweden would remain quite unknown. The English simply have no interest in us.

It is always said that the English are 'insular'. I find the expression misleading. The English friends I have acquired in London are all keen travellers. They seem always to be back from a visit to the United States, Canada, Australia or India; sometimes also Europe, but then mostly Paris, Berlin or Rome.

I have the feeling that England turns its back on northern Europe, particularly Scandinavia. The Norwegians imagine that English hearts beat warmly for Norway. If there really are English hearts beating for Norway, I guess the reason is the salmon fishing.

Among my friends in London was an Irishman, Maurice Healy, nephew of the famous Tim Healy, who for many years was one of the wittiest and most esteemed leaders of the Irish group in the House of Commons. I often met Tim Healy in Maurice's house in Wilton Place. Maurice was just as witty as his uncle, but he had no taste for politics. All the time he could spare from his work as a barrister he devoted to good food and above all good wines. Through Maurice I became a member of a private club where we tasted wines. I should perhaps explain that in my parents' house we were allowed from the age of fifteen to drink wine at dinner. My father used to ask me how the wine tasted and when he found that I could make fairly clear distinctions between one wine and another he was highly amused.

With his encouragement, I devoted some time to sampling his cellar, which was well stocked, particularly with claret. Therefore I was not entirely at a loss when I joined the private club in London. Ten or twelve of us met once every month, mostly in the Windham Club. We drank only claret. Every member offered one wine and it was his duty to present his wine with a short speech. One was expected to comment on the wine's qualities in a light, bantering way. The master of this particular art was the chairman of the club, Sir D. Plunket Barton, former Chief Justice of Ireland and author of an excellent biography of Bernadotte.

Maurice Healy had a special gift for this kind of speech-making. I remember him presenting an Haut Brion in a lyrical way, explaining its likeness to the character of the Irish. This was far from surprising, Maurice said, as his researches into the history of this famous château had shown that 'Haut Brion' was simply a corruption of the Irish 'O'Brien', a name glorious in Irish history and also the name of the first owner of the château near Bordeaux.

It was wonderful to listen to Maurice's after-dinner conversation with his Uncle Tim. It was always a display of Irish wit and repartee. It was rewarding to listen to old Tim's descriptions of the debates in the House of Commons before the First World War. It was really his reminiscences which inspired me to queue for a seat in the public gallery of the House during 1928 and 1929, when I listened to many debates. Winston Churchill was Chancellor of the Exchequer, but hardly inspiring in this role. On the Conservative side it was Stanley Baldwin whom I admired as a political leader and sometimes also as a debater. I will never forget how he wound up a debate of many days on the question of Tariffs, a debate of considerable difficulty for his party: 'I am not so much impressed by the differences of opinion,' he said, 'as by the many-sidedness of truth.'

The most superb speaker was, of course, Lloyd George. He had a voice which could dominate the whole Albert Hall with an audience of many thousands, but which he could lower to a whisper while the members of the House of Commons leaned forward with their hands at their ears in order to catch each word falling from the mouth of the old wizard.

I went to many dances that first spring. I remember particularly a ball at Lansdowne House in Berkeley Square, where the host was not Lord Lansdowne but somebody as unlike him as possible, Mr Selfridge. The owner of the great department store had rented Lansdowne House for a year.

It was really not the guests at the ball who fascinated me but the house. Lansdowne House, which was demolished a few years later, was an exquisite eighteenth-century mansion, built in the purest Adam style. It was surrounded by a large park. Between dances one walked in the illuminated park, with its groups of white marble statues, and could hardly believe one was right in the centre of London—and in the twentieth century.

Lady Dorothy Macmillan, whose father, the Duke of Devonshire, had married the daughter of the old Lord Lansdowne, told me that the park round Lansdowne House was connected by a little passage with the even larger park of her family's town house, Devonshire House, whose stately eighteenth-century façade dominated Piccadilly for a century and a half. It seemed astonishing to me that as late as the 1920s these two private houses and their grounds should occupy many acres of central London.

The dining-room of Devonshire House, Lady Dorothy told me, was so big that it was hardly comfortable to be less than thirty persons at table. Open house was kept in the best eighteenth-century style; relatives and friends could come to luncheon or dinner whenever they wanted. After luncheon they often played tennis; Devonshire House had two courts and if more were needed there were another two over at Lansdowne House.

After a few months in London I found that I had to move to a cheaper part of London. Towards the end of the 1920s London was the most expensive city in Europe. As an attaché I was paid £40 a month. My father had helped me amply in Paris but I didn't like to draw too much on his generosity.

There was another reason. Being constantly with English friends I had discovered that my English was not good enough. Everybody knows how important it is to speak proper French in France. Englishmen are so used to foreigners maltreating their language that one might get the impression that they are insensitive to foreigners' bad pronunciation and scant vocabulary. But if one intends to live for some time with Englishmen as friends it is, I think, necessary to make an effort to speak the language decently.

All this led me to look for a family with which I could live inexpensively and at the same time hear good English and practise my own. In due course I found a family where the father had an academic background and was willing to help me with my English. The family lived in a distant part of Kensington which probably had been almost fashionable at the end of the nineteenth century but since then had slipped down the social ladder.

The small brick houses in this district all looked alike; in the dark it was difficult to distinguish one from another. We were rather cramped in our house and in the mornings one had to queue for the bathroom. In spring and summer one could sit on a bench in the back yard, looking for a glimpse of the sun.

Here I lived for ten months. It was a very useful experience to live in a typical English middle-class household; one which was conservative, and steeped in traditional British values. The family newspaper was the *Daily Mail*, with its daily reports on the Royal Family and high society. It was incomprehensible to me why the very likeable young people in the family, all working in offices in the City, should devote such intense interest to the *Daily Mail*'s descriptions of society dinners and dances. They spoke of Lady X or Lord Y as if they knew the habits and the past history of these illustrious persons. Several times I attended dances which were described next morning in the *Daily Mail*. Of course I never told my friends in the family that I had been among the guests. This would have changed the atmosphere. But it was strange for me to sit at the breakfast table listening to their comments on the *Daily Mail*'s description of the leading guests at the ball.

There was obviously a strong element of snobbism in all this. But there was also something else, a definite need to enrich their own rather grey daily lives with visions of another, and a glittering, world.

Their intense interest in the Royal Family had, of course, much deeper motives. The daily discussions of the happenings at Court were an expression of their strong feeling of the unity of the Royal Family with the whole British people. 'The Royals' belonged to them all.

I also found it strange to listen to their discussions of different social classes and class differences. Often I heard them say: 'But he belongs to quite a different class.' Another expression which sticks in my mind was, 'But he's not exactly out of the top drawer'. I remember a show at a West End theatre in which there was a scene between a young couple who had just become engaged. They spoke of the schools where they had been educated, the church to which they belonged, the part of London where they lived, the English accent they preferred. At last they came to the well-considered conclusion that they both belonged to the 'upper-middle-middle-class'.

Some of these discussions of class and class distinctions were rather tiresome, but there was a pleasant side to it, I thought. There was no envy of the 'upper classes'. One of the great qualities of the English, it seemed to me, was their complete lack of envy.

Contemplating these English peculiarities I asked myself whether it is really right to speak only of classes. Rather, it seemed to me that the English have a natural instinct to form groups or circles. There are always some who belong to the inner circle and some who have been left outside. In an English pub there is always a group of regular customers with their special privileges. Later I was to discover that also the English industrial workers, particularly in the coal industry, have the same natural tendency to form groups.

[47]

At first I thought that what decided 'class' was, on the one hand, a man's family background and on the other his material resources. I was soon to find that this was a far too simple classification. There were infinitely more factors. Which school and university have you been to? This is perhaps the most important factor of all. Which sort of English do you speak? It is not only a question of accent but also of choice of words.

As a Swede, I was used to a more simple and straightforward social structure and I sometimes found the English peculiarities rather trying. At the same time I had to recognize that the extreme differentiation which is so typical of English society and English institutions has given them the richness of light and shade, of vivid contrasts, which have marked English political, social and literary life for centuries. The whole array of great English novelists could be called in as witnesses.

A few months after my arrival in London, my chief, the Consul-General, told me that I shouldn't 'waste my time' with consular business. Instead I was to write reports on economic and social problems in Britain. What interested my chief was British industry. I had to write reports on the British steel, paper and coal industries. One day I said it seemed absurd to sit in London and write about industries I had never seen. He gave me full freedom to travel as much as I wanted, but at my own expense.

So for about four months I travelled round England to study industry on the spot. I was helped by the numerous Swedish Consuls and also by leading businessmen I met; but most rewarding of all was to live among the industrial workers themselves.

The dominating problem of the time was the situation of the coal industry after the great strike of 1926. I devoted much time to studying all the elaborate reports produced by the various commissions of enquiry. I then went to stay for a time in one of the relatively modern coalfield areas in Northumberland. I spent the first night at an inn right in the middle of the village. While I was having a glass of beer I got into conversation with some miners and this led to my moving into their house near by. There was the mother, a widow, and three sons—all miners. The three men worked on different shifts, so they were seldom all at home together.

I slept on a sofa in a sort of parlour or sitting-room. The family belonged to the 'upper' working class. They told me proudly that they had worked in the mine for generations. It took a day or two before they opened up. Miners are a world apart. It was Guinness's good stout which brought us together. They told stories for hours. Not much about their work and the mine, but mostly about betting, horse-racing and dog-racing. When I started to speak of the coal industry they merely said that they were happy not to be in such a mess as the miners in Wales. They didn't hide their misgivings about the Conservative Government (which they blamed for the great strike three years before). They hinted that the miners had a friend in the Prince of Wales, and my room was decorated with a portrait of the Prince.

In Sweden we have always attached great importance to the idea of equality. Swedes insist that everybody should be equal to everybody else. When I spent my evenings with my miner friends I was struck by their lack of interest in equality. That the owner of the coal mine was probably a millionaire didn't seem to them worthy of comment. That the workers in many other English industries were much better paid seemed to them to belong to the natural order of things. 'Miners have always been badly paid,' they said with a smile. It was only now that I understood Chesterton's sally that the English working man is less interested in the equality of men than in the inequality of horses.

It would be wrong to think that this lack of interest in equality is a sign of resignation. If the English workers—as I learned to know them—did not feel strongly about equality they were certainly ready to stand up vigorously for liberty and justice. When my miner friends spoke about the injustices they had suffered at the time of the great strike they were definitely in a fighting mood.

From Northumberland I went to Wales and spent three days in Ebbw Vale. For many years this area had suffered from mass unemployment, and it was the most distressing scene I had ever witnessed: endless rows of small brick houses with sooted walls; everywhere groups of unemployed men queuing for food at canteens; hungry children in rags. All this, which I observed for three days with an increasingly heavy heart, had been going on for more than three years.

For the first time in my life I was overwhelmed by indignation at social injustice. Could one imagine a more unjust, a more inhuman

D [49]

system than this, where hundreds of thousands of workers were left in hunger and distress while some of the landowners, who had never made any active contribution to the coal industry, enjoyed incomes of millions? There must be, I told myself, something fundamentally wrong with an economic system which led to such consequences.*

The impression Ebbw Vale made on me was so strong that my whole thinking about the English economy took a much more critical turn.

Nobody who tried to analyze the problems of cost in the English export industries could avoid the conclusion that the rate of the pound sterling had been fixed too high in relation to the dollar. It was Churchill who took this decision in 1925 and the English economy had been suffering the consequences ever since. But quite apart from the monetary aspect it seemed clear to me that the British economy suffered from a number of traditional defects. One could, of course, doubt whether the nationalization of the railways and the mines was the right answer. What was certain, however, was that a great deal more enterprise and willingness to invest were badly needed.

My impression was that the British financiers in their palatial headquarters in the City of London had their eyes fixed on the far-flung possessions of the British Empire, while they turned their backs on the British home industries. It was easier to find millions for the development of the steel industry in Canada or India, or for the oil industry in Burma, than to find money for the British railways or coal mines.

I always had a deep dislike of everything smacking of imperialism. I used to maintain that men like Joseph Chamberlain and Lord Milner were really not English.

Some years earlier E. M. Forster had written his masterly novel *A Passage to India*. This book, which focused on the relationship between the British Raj and the natives of India, was widely read during the latter part of the 1920s. Would this not persuade millions of Englishmen that the end of the British domination of India was in sight? This was the question that I posed in my youthful zest for opposition.

* From 1948 until his untimely death Hugh Gaitskell was a friend of mine. I once told him of my visit to Ebbw Vale. Gaitskell then told me that it was when he first visited Ebbw Vale that he decided to join the Labour Party.

Obviously I had come to engage myself much more deeply in English problems than I had done with the French. This was partly a result of a deepening political interest. But it was probably even more the result of my steadily increasing attraction to the English and the English way of life.

One clear morning in December 1929, as I saw the English coast disappear while my ship steamed eastwards across the North Sea, I felt sure that a great deal of myself would for ever be attached to England.

IV

Moscow

When I was on holiday in Sweden during the summer of 1929 Mr Richert, the head of personnel in the Foreign Ministry,* told me that I was due to leave London at the end of the year. He asked if I had any preferences as to my next assignment. I answered immediately, 'Moscow'. Richert said that this was easy to arrange as nobody had ever before expressed a wish to be sent there.

My father had often talked to me about Russia. 'If I hadn't been tied to Sweden in so many ways,' he used to say, 'I would have gone to Russia as a young man and gone into business there'. He did, in fact, visit Russia many times in later years.

My own interest in Sweden's great neighbour on the East was very much influenced by the passion I had, even as a schoolboy, for Russian literature. At school I wrote an essay on the philosophy of history in Tolstoy's *War and Peace*.

With Tolstoy as my starting point and centre, I had made long excursions into the Russian literature of the nineteenth century: Turgenev, Gogol, Gontcharov and others. Some distance apart from these summits there was the dark mountain mass of Dostoievsky; I did some climbing there, but found the perspectives so staggering that I soon came down again—a frightened little bourgeois. It was only later that I had the courage to make any long excursion into the world of Dostoievsky.

Russian literature had led me to a study of Russian history. *War and Peace* made me concentrate on the period of Alexander I and particularly the question of Finland. I felt more and more that the traditional Swedish interpretation of the Russian attitude to Scandinavia was misleading. King Oscar II had spoken of Russia's 'longing' towards the sea as a 'law of nature' which would lead Russia to attempt to dominate Scandinavia, and so reach the Atlantic. But did this longing really exist?

On a cold morning in January 1930 I left Stockholm to travel East

* Arvid Richert (born 1887), Swedish diplomat. Permanent Under-Secretary, 1934–7; Minister in Berlin, 1937–45.

for the first time in my life. A journey to Moscow at this time was rather unusual, almost a journey of exploration.

I had to promise my father to write long letters home, which in due course I did. So much has been written about the Soviet Union in the forty-odd years since then that what I had to say is not of any importance but here are a few purely personal extracts:

Moscow, January 13, 1930

Here I sit in a hotel opposite the Kremlin. I would like to tell Mother and yourself of my journey.

In Helsingfors I was received in a friendly way in the Legation. I went round the centre of the city, which I found more beautiful than I had expected. This is to a fairly large extent the merit of the period of Alexander I.

The train was very slow to reach Leningrad. There I was met by our Consul, Ytterberg, a round, rosy-cheeked and very friendly man. He and his chauffeur guided me through an immense crowd of people surrounding the Finland Station. Ytterberg tells me it is the same everywhere in Russia: people standing and waiting. For what?

You have often spoken of the stately Petersburg. It surpassed all my expectations. You would surely recognize much from the time before the Revolution. It is true that the great palaces are closed and that no elegant people are seen. But was it not so also before the Revolution that the life in the streets was dominated by the great grey mass of people? Anyhow, this is the case today.

All women wear shawls, threadbare black or grey coats—if they have any coats at all—and boots of felt or shoes of bass (rope). One has the impression of a lack of clothing, lack of food—and lack of happiness. One doesn't have to go many steps from the magnificent main streets to find oneself in dark areas of utter misery. I was looking for some of the streets in *Crime and Punishment*. In fact this whole quarter of the city is one great Dostoievsky landscape.

There is a new and very visible upper-class. They are the young Communists of both sexes, easy to recognize by their leather jackets and black boots. They are very full of themselves and people are rather frightened of them.

In my compartment on the Moscow train there was someone asleep in the upper berth. When the ticket collector came round he asked me a question which I didn't understand. Suddenly the man in the upper berth started to speak fluent Russian. When the collector left us we shook hands and I found he was the famous Lindgren, head of the Swedish electrical factories in Jaroslav. We sat down with a bottle of vodka and talked most of the night. He really knows Russia!

It has been a magnificent feat to build those huge factories in the midst of a chaotic economy and transportation system. Lindgren says that the Russian administrative apparatus is so clumsy that it often takes half a year to get a decision which was needed months before. Another difficulty is the lack of skilled labour. There is an unlimited abundance of young men from the countryside who are looking for jobs in industry, but they have no experience beyond ploughing with oxen and harvesting corn.

Suddenly Lindgren jumped up to shut the window. 'There are *bezspironiki*—orphans—everywhere,' he said. 'They hang around the railway stations and climb on the roofs of trains. They are unbelievably clever at picking up clothes or anything in the compartments.'

When I expressed my compassion with these so-called 'wild children' (I had seen a few groups of them at the stations in Leningrad) Lindgren said they had become a great plague. Nobody knows even approximately how many there are. Four or five years ago they were estimated at some two millions. Since then many have died of sickness, lack of food, clothing and care. Some have been shot by the police when chasing them after a burglary or a murder. It is a terrifying story.

You know my chief here, Carl von Heidenstam, but I had never seen him before. His looks are very English, his fresh, rosy complexion contrasting with his whitening hair. His way of speaking of my future work is also very English. He has a pleasant, casual way when discussing people and situations. He was particularly keen to know about the situation in England after the elections. After listening for a while he said that he intended to take me along to see Litvinov, who is the real Foreign Minister (although Tjitjenin remains the nominal Minister).

Moscow, January 25, 1930

Now I have had a little more time to get to know Moscow. It has nothing of the monumental beauty of Leningrad; it is a gigantic village which has grown at random. Only God knows how many churches there are in Moscow and although many are now very ramshackle many are kept up fairly well by the faithful. One sees thousands going to church.

There are few motor-cars and very little to buy in the shops. Soviet bigwigs and foreign diplomats have access to special shops where one finds all sorts of *delicatessen*.

I think the worst part is the housing problem. From my windows I can see straight into an apartment house. There they live eight or ten in each room.

The diplomatic corps is, of course, far smaller than in Paris. One gets to know most of them fairly soon. Heidenstam is good enough to take me along. We play badminton almost every afternoon in the attractive Italian embassy. There is Heidenstam, the Italian Ambassador, Cerutti (who looks like Caesar Augustus), a secretary, Staffeti, and myself. After the badminton we take tea in Madame Cerutti's drawing-room. She is Hungarian by origin and has been, I believe, a great actress. In any case she dominates the conversation at the tea table, where all the Italian diplomats and their wives are present (they all live in the same house). Cerutti and Heidenstam sit in a corner exchanging information and discussing the political questions of the day.

I have got to know Hilger, one of the German counsellors, who is generally considered to be the greatest expert on Russian economic problems. In his house we have a lot of fun. The other night there was a fancy-dress ball and I was dressed as a Cossack, not very original, but I had succeeded in finding a pair of red Cossack boots and this decided the matter. We danced till well into the morning. Then I couldn't get out of my boots. I changed into ordinary clothes but my red boots showed below my trousers. Heidenstam asked me to come to his office because of a report he wanted me to write. I tried to hide my boots, but Heidenstam discovered them and had a good laugh.

On Sundays we go ski-ing. Usually it is Heidenstam, the Italians and I who drive out to a farm on the Moscow plain where we keep our skis. It is not exactly exciting ski-ing country, but perhaps this is as well, because some of the Italians are beginners. Madame Cerutti goes into the attack on a downhill slope shouting 'Viva

Savoia!' but usually I have to help her up afterwards. At a distance, a group of Russian peasants watch our strange proceedings. They have never seen skis before. When we speak to them they mumble in their beards. They don't like any new inventions.

There was no British Embassy in Moscow at this time. I had several friends in the French Embassy, but relations between the French and the Soviets were rather strained. My best and closest contact was with the German Embassy, which was undoubtedly the best informed of all the diplomatic missions in Moscow.

I described an example of the Soviet-German co-operation in a letter to my father:

The other night I had a remarkable experience. I was invited to supper by the German military attaché. When I reached the gate of his house I found there was a massive police guard. There are, of course, policemen outside every diplomatic house in Moscow, but this time it seemed to be a solid wall of men from the GPU.

I discovered the reason when I entered the reception room. Aside from the other guests—only German and Russian officers and a few of the German counsellors and secretaries—there stood two men. One of them I recognized immediately. It was General Budjonny, with his wavy moustaches. The other was a strongly built man of medium height wearing a white Russian peasant's dress and black boots. A big head, dark moustache, low forehead and penetrating eyes. It took me a few seconds to realize that this was in fact Stalin himself, the real master of Russia.

At supper we sat at long tables. Stalin, who never let himself be separated from Budjonny, sat at the head of the table I was at. The German military attaché, who speaks perfect Russian, tried to make conversation with the great man but without much success. Instead it was Budjonny who told stories of the heroic deeds of the Red Cavalry during the Civil War and the war in Poland. Budjonny is a former Tsarist non-commissioned officer. I couldn't understand much of what he said, but it must have been quite amusing as Stalin roared with laughter and slapped his knees. There was a great deal of drinking at our table and it was, of course, Budjonny who took the lead. Stalin's own contribution to the conversation was when he now and then pointed his finger at Budjonny shouting: 'Look at him—how he drinks! The old drunkard.' Then he roared with laughter again.

Immediately after supper Stalin left, explaining that he had to go back to the Kremlin to work. It seems that his real working hours are during the night. But I also had the impression that Stalin was happy to leave. He didn't like us Westerners. He looks, in fact, rather oriental.

By the time I had been a month or two in Moscow I was absorbed in speculation about the real situation in the Soviet Union. There were always rumours of splits within the Communist Party or revolts in various parts of the country. Such rumours coloured many political dispatches during the 1920s, not least the reports of my chief. The Italian and Polish Ambassadors gave us—in the strictest confidence, of course—information about troubles in the Ukraine or about Trotsky's intrigues to split the Communist Party.

There was also much talk about opposition to the régime within the Red Army. My German friends did not exclude the possibility that these rumours might be right, but they always pointed out that we had no real proof. What we could see with our own eyes—and the Germans had many eyes in Russia—was that the régime held the people under firm control. Hilger often pointed out that change could come only from within the ruling party.

I was eager to see something of Russia outside Moscow. The opportunity came when a German engineer whom I often met at Hilger's was going on a journey round the district of Tula in order to inspect agricultural machinery delivered by his firm in Germany. In a letter to my father I described this, my first journey into the Russian countryside:

I have just come back from a journey in the district of Tula. What strikes one first is the deplorable condition of the roads. If we hadn't had a very strong car we would never have been able to do it. For long stretches the so-called road is simply open fields. Often the 'road' is some fifty metres wide. I suppose this is because cars have tried to avoid the beaten track.

Having read so many Russian novels à la Tolstoy or Turgenev I had a romantic image of the Russian village. The reality is very different. Perhaps this is because of the Civil War, the years of famine at the beginning of the 1920s, and the general disorder which seems to mark the life of the Russian countryside. The peasants' huts seem not to have been repaired for the last ten or fifteen years. Often windows are missing, as window glass is unobtainable. In their place pieces of wood or dirty rags have been put in.

Usually we lodged with the priests. They live, as a rule, hardly better than the peasants, but one likes to believe that they keep their houses a bit cleaner, though I'm not really sure if this is true. By the second day I had to chase bugs on my body.

My German friend curses and is furious. Most of the machinery delivered by his firm is in need of repair already, after only one year. The peasants are not used to the handling of machinery. They are slow and obstinate. But they are true to their own characters. Strangers rarely visit their villages, and it is much more of a sensation when the visitors are foreigners. The peasants make no distinction between various kinds of foreigners; they call them all 'German'.

Soon after we have established ourselves in the priest's house a group of peasants—probably the elders of the village—arrive and knock on the door. They treat the priest with no special reverence. He is one of them. My German friend has brought along a considerable supply of vodka so he can give plenty of drink to the peasants. This loosens their tongues. I am far from understanding everything they say, but my German friend explains afterwards.

They ask questions about the agricultural machinery. This leads them to complain about the authorities—bad planning, lack of tools, high prices; it is a real lamentation.

But somehow I have the feeling that these peasants have always been complaining, without ever expecting that their complaints will lead to any results. There is a sense of timelessness as they sit around us, with their unkempt beards, their clothes worn to rags and their dirty rope shoes.

When the village is situated near what was once a great estate my friend sometimes asks how it happened that the manor house was burnt down. The peasants describe, without a trace of shame, how they burned down the house and cut down the trees in the park. Anyhow, they repeat, 'The land belongs to us'.

When I think that the peasant population of Russia numbers more than 150 million, I wonder how much time will have to pass before the Communist régime will be able to put some order into the agriculture.

You can't imagine the *tristesse* of the Russian village!

My depressing impressions of the Russian countryside did not prevent me from enjoying the coming of spring in Moscow. It was a late spring and it came quite abruptly. After all the months of snow and darkness it was suddenly bright and sunny. I remember a day when, walking along Tverskaja, I suddenly felt totally bowled over by the light and the air; never have I felt the arrival of spring so intensely.

I had at last found an apartment. It formed part of a big house on the outskirts of Moscow and belonged to a Danish-owned telegraph company. In the house lived one of the directors, a Scotsman by the name of Cunningham. I only saw him when he practised golf shots in the garden. As no golf-course existed in Moscow, Cunningham played golf by himself on the broad main road to Smolensk.

I had a corner of the house to myself. An old woman cleaned and cooked for me, but she lived with her family somewhere in the neighbourhood. The first time I went down in the evening to the kitchen, which was in the basement, I discovered to my horror, rows of black *tarachani*—cockroaches—marching on the kitchen floor. With a log from the fire I killed some thirty of them. The following morning my servant looked rather grim. 'You have killed my *tarachani*,' she said. 'Yes,' I answered, 'they are abominable creatures.'

'Absolutely not,' the old woman retorted. 'The black *tarachani* are good and keep the room clean. The red ones are bad and fight. We call them *Schvedi* [Swedes].'

I was sure the old woman had no idea that I was a Swede, so I couldn't take it amiss. When I told the story to Hilger, who knew more Russian than most Russians, he said that my servant must come from some very distant and backward part of Russia where they still gave warlike animals their old names. In most parts of Russia, the cockroaches were now called *Prussiaki*—Prussians.

Through my German friends I got to know a fair number of Russians, but the police were very vigilant. One always had to assume that Russians who accepted one's invitations had received permission from the police and were supposed to report back to them. A Russian woman I knew well confessed to me that she had to report once a week to the police and that she found it a great strain always to invent something new to tell them.

Nevertheless I saw a great deal of my Russian friends. One day when I was having luncheon with some of them two young men rushed into the room. Great emotion, many kisses and embraces. These two had been arrested some months before, and their friends had more or less resigned themselves to the thought that they would never be seen again. Now they told us in great excitement that they had been released from the Liubljanka prison only an hour ago. No explanation had been given. They had spent several months in that great prison in the centre of Moscow.

At first they had been questioned night after night. It was evident that the police wanted to make them confess that they had had secret relations with White Russians in Paris. One of the two was a young Prince Lvov, a relative of the former prime minister. After two weeks of questioning they had been left alone for some weeks; then the questionings had started again.

The strangest experience, they said, was the daily walk through the corridors of the prison, when they saw hundreds of people who had long been considered dead by the outside world—General K., Senator G., the journalist P. and many others. Nobody was allowed to say a word. They could only glance at each other.

The year 1930 was only ten years away from the most difficult years of the Revolution. There were, of course, some Russians who liked to talk of their sufferings during the first years of the Revolution. But the great majority avoided speaking of that terrible period— the famine, the splitting up of families and the police terror. They didn't care to look back; it was difficult enough to go on.

So much had happened in the thirteen years since the Revolution that the minds of many Russians had suffered more than they could bear. Time before the Revolution had disappeared behind the horizon of their memories.

This was important, I thought, when one tried to make an assessment of the stability of the régime. In Western Europe there was so much whispering of a Tsarist restoration. I had met many white Russian emigrés in the drawing-room of Countess Ehrensvärd. One evening in Paris I had heard Field-Marshal Mannerheim express himself in a way which gave me the firm impression that a White Russian restoration was by no means impossible. But in Moscow I found that one could not live more than a few months in this centre of Communist Russia without realizing that all speculations about the restoration of a Tsarist régime were very wide of the mark.

During the summer of 1930 I went by train to Nishni Novgorod to catch a steamboat for a journey on the Volga to Astrakhan. In the next compartment of the train I found my friend the German military attaché. He told me that he too was on his way to Nishni. He was to visit the factories which were building tanks and aeroplanes for both the Red Army and the German Reichswehr. The Treaty of Versailles had deprived Germany of the right to possess these arms. So now they were being built in Russia for the Germans.

The military attaché spoke quite openly about this. He said that it would have taken the Russians many years to build modern aeroplanes and tanks, so the German technicians had probably speeded up Russian rearmament by five or six years.

The Volga steamboat I boarded at Nishni was divided into four classes, exactly as before the Revolution. On the lower afterdeck hundreds of people were huddled together without shelter against wind or rain. On the top deck we had large cabins which would have been very comfortable if there hadn't been so many vermin.

One would need the pen of a Tolstoy or a Paustovsky to describe the mighty Volga. I remember a morning when we stood on the upper deck watching the equally mighty River Kama join the Volga. I have seldom seen a sight in nature of such power and magnitude. The groups of peasants and their families patiently waiting at the landing stages presented probably very much the same picture as they would have done fifty or a hundred years before. One group of grave-faced men, bowing and kneeling in unison, caused me to wonder for a while before I realized that they were Tartars who, as good Muslims, were saying their prayers in the direction of Mecca.

One day the Captain came to see me. He knew that I had tickets to Astrakhan, but he wanted to warn me that there was famine all the way from Samara; it would be impossible to provide us with food. He strongly advised me to disembark at Samara and catch a train back to Moscow. I followed his advice, although I was inclined to believe that the real reason for his warning was that the secret police didn't like a foreign diplomat, even a minor one, going to Stalingrad and its gigantic new tractor factories.

When I disembarked at Samara I could see almost immediately that the warning of an impending famine was well justified. Most shops were closed and those that were not had long queues of people with grey, staring faces. I walked around for an hour trying to find an hotel. They were all closed. At last I told myself that the best I could do was to speak to the GPU, the security police. It was easy enough to find their headquarters; everybody in Samara seemed to know. It was even easier to reach the head of the police. He told me he had been waiting for me for the last hour. He gave me tea while he explained the situation. His advice was that I should leave Samara at once. The ordinary trains were overcrowded and would probably take three or four days to reach Moscow. My best bet was to stop a military train, carrying troops from Turkestan, which would probably pass through Samara that evening.

Escorted by heavily-armed police, I left the headquarters for the railway station which, as in most Russian provincial cities, was quite a distance away. As we approached the station I saw a great crowd— men, women and children—lying on the ground. The disorder and dirt were unbelievable. These were peasant families who had been driven out of their villages during the campaign for the collectivization of agriculture, started by Stalin in the spring of 1930. The peasants had been told that they and their families were going to find new land in Siberia. They had walked endlessly in sun and heat, expecting to find a train at Samara which would take them to the promised land in Siberia.

They had believed the assurances given to them by the Soviet administration. Now they were lying on the open ground without a chance of even getting near the trains. There seemed to be no food. Small children wailed; women sat with their heads in their hands weeping; men broke out now and then with desperate shouts of hunger and fury. Outside the station the soldiers of the GPU were lined up with their machine-guns.

I was hidden in a room near the railway track. We sat there until ten o'clock in the evening when a gigantic train rolled in. The policemen lifted me up to a carriage in the middle of the train. This carriage was for the officers of the regiment, and they received me with true Russian hospitality, gave me a late supper and even served me some Caucasian wine.

The news of the arrival of this strange guest spread rapidly, so I was soon surrounded by as many officers as the spacious compartment could hold. The officers were obviously happy to find somebody who could talk to them about Moscow and the food situation, the opera and the ballet. They told me they had been almost two years in Turkestan, engaged in a campaign which seemed to have been both vast and tough. I got the impression that several divisions had been engaged. (It is typical of the difficulties of information that the numerous military attachés in Moscow apparently had no inkling of this quite important military campaign.)

The following day we were all very gay. The regimental chorus sang through its whole repertoire; we had egg-and-spoon races along the corridors. Suddenly there appeared a man of about thirty, wearing not the standard military uniform but a black leather jacket. He was the *politruk*, the Communist commissar, or political officer, of the regiment. He had obviously been told about me in advance, for he said immediately, 'You are a Swede and a diplomat'. When I said that was so, he declared that ever since the Swedish kings had ceased to attack Russia there had been friendship between the Swedish and the Russian peoples. He said this in a rather loud voice as the officers had crowded round us to listen. I confirmed the mutual friendship. 'But,' exclaimed the *politruk*, 'it is therefore all the more deplorable that the imperialistic and capitalistic circles in Sweden plan an attack on the Soviet people.'

I answered that Sweden had, on the contrary, disarmed. Had the Soviet Union done the same? The *politruk* ignored my question and continued to criticize Sweden. Addressing the assembled officers rather than me, he said that a Swedish Commission under General Ackerman had put forward proposals to increase the Swedish Army and Air Force with a view to making war on the Soviet Union. This was in line with events in Finland, where the aggressive forces in power were now pressing for an attack on Russia.

I answered that this was pure nonsense. Sweden and Finland were small states which only wanted peace and security. And so on . . .

The following morning we arrived in Moscow. After two hours of cleaning myself of vermin, I reported for duty at the Legation.

[63]

My chief had for a long time been asking for a transfer to a country where he and his family could live properly, pointing out that there was no suitable school in Moscow for his children. So in the summer of 1930 von Heidenstam left to become Minister in Constantinople.

As his successor, Baron Gyllenstierna, then Counsellor in London, was appointed. Gyllenstierna was one of the great feudal land-owners of southern Sweden, but nevertheless he was a man of liberal ideas and in his private life something of a bohemian.

We had just asked the Soviet Government for their agreement to the appointment of Gyllenstierna as Minister in Moscow when *Isvestia* published a story from Stockholm about an interview he was said to have given to a well-known Swedish journalist in London. He was reported to have declared that there was still hope for a change of régime in the Soviet Union, adding that it was possible that a push from the outside would be necessary to achieve this change.

Our acting *chargé d'affaires* in Moscow, Mr Wilhelm Assarsson, and I read and re-read the report in *Isvestia*. We were aghast. How could we now hope to get the Soviet Government's agreement to his nomination?

First, of course, it was absolutely imperative to issue a categorical denial of the whole report. Then Gyllenstierna was persuaded to make some declarations of friendship towards Russia. At last Assarsson went to see Litvinov. He gave a full description of Gyllenstierna's background and personality. Litvinov showed more interest in the Shakespearian Guildenstern than in his present-day descendent. Assarsson told me afterwards that he had the distinct impression that the Soviet Government felt a certain snobbish satisfaction that Sweden was sending to Moscow a nobleman of such ancient lineage. 'If the British would send a Duke of Norfolk or Devonshire,' he said, 'the Russians would beam with pleasure.'

The Russian agreement to Gyllenstierna's appointment was soon forthcoming.

I had now spent more than six months in Moscow and I tried very hard to come to some sort of general conclusion as to the situation in the Soviet Union. This was, of course, the subject of incessant and often passionate discussion in Western Europe and the United

States. Bertrand Russell had resolutely condemned the Bolshevik régime. André Gide had presented himself as the enthusiastic protagonist of the Soviet society. The foreign correspondents in Moscow were divided into different and often opposite schools. One could sit listening into the early hours of the morning when the witty American correspondent, Walter Duranty, explained away even the most obvious defects of the Soviet system.

I was eager to listen, but more and more I became convinced that one seldom, if ever, arrives at sound judgments of given situations if one approaches them from ideological premisses. I remembered that William James had insisted that one had first to enquire *why* one was searching for a truth before doing the searching.

When I was sitting in Moscow pondering about the Soviet Union it was not to find out whether the Soviet régime corresponded to the principles of democracy; that it didn't do so was quite obvious. The surprising thing was that so many otherwise quite intelligent Western observers had succeeded in persuading themselves to the contrary.

The purpose of my thinking was to come to a conclusion about the future importance of the Soviet Union to Sweden. This meant that I had, firstly, to come to some sort of judgment about the probable future of the Soviet régime for at least the next ten years, and, secondly, to form an opinion on the Soviets' foreseeable attitude to the outside world, particularly Scandinavia.

I have already explained that, after a few months in Russia, it seemed to me fairly obvious that a Tsarist restoration was out of the question. It was only in White Russian circles in Berlin, London or Paris that this was discussed as a possibility. So where could a threat to the Bolshevik régime come from?

When the Bolsheviks seized power in 1917 there were only 35,000 members of the Bolshevik Party. That this comparatively small group had been able to establish themselves as masters of a people of 180 millions could be explained by the fact that they had the support of the peasants, who wanted to possess the land and to end the war. The Bolsheviks promised them both.

Once established in the big cities, a Russian ruler can dominate the whole vast country. This is demonstrated by all Russian history.

Many foreign observers in the 1920s speculated about the

E   [65]

possibility of a seizure of power by the Army. It was often said that the Russian revolution must end like the French, in a military dictatorship. A new Napoleon. My German friends, who had far closer relations with the Red Army than anybody else, assured me that there were no such tendencies among the Russian officers. Moreover, the Communist Party had its spies and controllers everywhere.

Thus one came to the conclusion which I had heard my friend Hilger proclaim many times, that a threat against the existing régime could only come from within the Communist Party itself. But this would only mean that one Communist group would replace another.

Anybody who had followed Stalin's rise to supreme power, his extraordinary dexterity and his complete lack of scruples, would find it difficult to believe that he would not be able to maintain his position for a long time. I came, therefore, to the conclusion that we had to allow for a continuation of the Bolshevik régime a long way into the future.

This was a purely political calculation. There was, however, a school of experts on Russia who tried to prove that even if the Bolshevik régime was politically strong the development of the Russian economy was so catastrophic that it was impossible to forecast a long life for Bolshevik Russia. Professor Karlgren had made a very knowledgeable analysis of the economy in his book *Bolshevik Russia*, which had made a profound impression in Sweden and the whole of Scandinavia.

My own studies of the Russian economy had led me to another conclusion. It was certainly true that the Bolsheviks had made great mistakes in many of their plans and that the human and material losses had been enormous. I had seen the Russian countryside. But nobody could deny that the total Russian production was rising, that heavy industry was developing rapidly and that the number of engineers and skilled workers had been multiplied many times over.

I was writing an analysis of the first Five-Year Plan. Having seen a great deal of the British economy, I was inclined to believe in the necessity for *some* central planning. With the help of my German friends, I tried to prove that the Russian economy had a future. When my study of Russia touched on psychological and political matters I kept in close contact with my immediate chief, Assarsson.

It is true that our methods were very different. I had to read a great deal of Russian history, economic statistics and studies made by German experts. Assarsson worked on intuition. He took his morning stroll through the streets of Moscow contemplating the people. He went for walks in the countryside and managed somehow to get the peasants and their children to talk to him.

It was very stimulating to discuss these wider perspectives with him. The attitude of almost all Swedish diplomats to Russia was dominated by ideological principles. But not Assarsson. After many discussions we agreed in general about the future of the Soviet Union—what he called our 'general line', a favourite expression of Stalin's.

If one assumed that this 'general line' was right, the next task was to consider the probable attitude of the Soviet Government to the outside world. Stalin had proclaimed the principle of the realization of Communism within one country, Russia. He tried to keep free from foreign conflicts and complications while strengthening his own country's economy, means of transportation and military defences. But was it not likely that if he succeeded in these policies we would have in ten years a Russia with an economic and military system so strengthened that a renewed Russian expansion would seem inevitable? This was, in fact, my conclusion. After the First World War and during the Revolution, Russia had been pushed back to frontiers which the country was hardly likely to accept in the long term. I thought particularly of Bessarabia, the eastern provinces of Poland and the small Baltic states. The most important consideration for a Swede was Russia's relationship to Finland.

For six weeks in the autumn of 1930 I served as Consul in Leningrad. I was again carried away by the beauty of this truly imperial city—the splendour of the many imperial palaces, the dark back streets of Raskolnikov, the spire of the fortress of Peter-Paul at sunset, and above all the dreamlike September nights.

But even if I could sit dreaming half the night at the windows of our house above the Neva, I still could not avoid wondering about the position of this strange city. Certainly it was one of the gravest decisions ever made by a Tsar when Peter the Great gave orders to build the future capital in a swamp at the extreme north-west corner of his immense empire. Peter had remarked that 'the women in Petersburg sleep badly because the frontier is so near', and ever since the Russian Government had been worried about the security of the capital. The two attacks made by Sweden-Finland in the course of the eighteenth century increased this Russian preoccupation. Alexander I could not resist the temptation to seize a favourable opportunity to defeat the weakened Swedish kingdom and to conquer Finland. But he did not absorb the conquered country, instead it was given full autonomy and, in fact, began to prosper economically because of the new access to the vast Russian market. What Alexander wanted was to obtain control of Finland from a military and foreign policy point of view, in the interests of the security of his capital, Petersburg.

It was during those weeks of September that I thought I had come to a proper understanding of the remarkable involvement of the vast Russian Empire in the destinies of Finland, which for so many centuries had been united to Sweden.

V

Stockholm

By the time I returned to Stockholm from Moscow in January 1931 I was fully involved in the Swedish diplomatic service. My father, who had earlier taken a rather sceptical view of my diplomatic career, had now changed his opinion. I lived with my parents and we resumed our family life, with concerts, regular visits to the opera, wine-tasting competitions between my father and myself and weekends at my parents' country house.

The later half of the 1920s had been a prosperous time for Sweden. I found that the atmosphere in Stockholm had changed. People spent much more money. There still was a Stockholm society, in which everybody had known everybody else since childhood, but the dinners and dances were now more opulent, though hardly more amusing.

The Social-Democrats had fallen from power in 1926. Thereafter we had governments changing every two years, governments mostly of Liberal, one time even of Conservative, complexion. Apart from the economic and social questions, there was one problem which remained in the centre of the political debate, the military organization of the country. The parties of the Left had a long anti-militarist tradition behind them. In 1925 the Socialist Government had radically cut down the Army and the Navy. The Air Force had hardly been born.

The short-lived Conservative Government had tried to persuade the Parliament to adopt a long-term plan for the country's military defences but had failed to get the necessary support. A weak Liberal Government, which had to rely sometimes on help from the Left, sometimes on support from the Right, was now in power. They did what most governments do when they want to avoid decisions: they appointed a Commission to study the question of the military defences.

I was asked to serve on the Commission as an 'expert' on Russia. It was, of course, absurd for me to be classified as an expert after serving only one year in Russia, but as my friend Westman reminded me, 'in the country of the blind the one-eyed man is king'. Anyhow, it gave me an opportunity to expound my ideas on Russia to a very representative group of politicians and military men.

The chairman was Mr Per Albin Hansson,* the leader of the Social-Democrat Party. He was a remarkable man. Born in a poor family in southern Sweden, he had first earned his living as an errand-boy and worked his way up to become a journalist in the Socialist press. He had in his youth been a radical anti-militarist, but with mature judgment he had come to realize that Sweden needed a national defence system.

He was a heavily-built man who enjoyed his food and drink, and even more a good laugh at an amusing story. In parliamentary politics he was a skilled tactician. The Swedish workers loved him, and slowly but surely he gained the confidence also of the industrialists and the bankers.

To me he was touchingly friendly. He listened to my talk about Russia and said afterwards that he would like us to have a free and personal discussion on the whole matter at a dinner which he organized himself in one of the old-fashioned restaurants of Stockholm. He had worked as a journalist abroad, particularly in England, but he was very cautious in his judgments on foreign countries and foreign policies. He liked to put blunt, large but seemingly simple questions, such as, 'Well, young fellow, tell me, is Stalin really popular with the Russian masses?' or 'Why are the Germans so active in Russia?' One day he asked me why I was advocating a big increase in Swedish armaments when I didn't believe Russia had any military plans against Sweden. I said I believed that a relatively prosperous country like Sweden had a duty to maintain proper defence, not because we were, at the moment, threatened by anybody but because the world situation was fluid and things might change. Moreover we had a duty to take our part in applying sanctions, if called upon, under the charter of the League of Nations.

Per Albin laughed and said that with such general arguments he would be quite unable to rally his party in support of a specific

* Per Albin Hansson was Minister of Defence 1920–3, 1925–6; became Prime Minister in 1932 and remained in this post (except for a few months) until his death in 1946.

programme for the defence budget. Therefore what he had to do was persuade the majority of them to accept a positive defence *policy*. He succeeded in the end, but much time was lost. It was only in the latter half of the 1930s that Sweden began to rearm, and even then rather slowly.

My studies in Russian economy led to other contacts. Ivar Kreuger, the head of the Swedish match company, asked me to come and see him. In fact, I had known Kreuger when I was a child.

The making of safety matches was an old industry in Sweden. Factories were scattered all over the south of the country. About the beginning of the century a number of these small factories were merged in one company and my father was president of the board; Ivar Kreuger was the managing director. In those days Kreuger often came to dinner with my parents. He was a shy man who said little. We children liked him and he used to walk with me in our garden in the country.

After my father left the board Kreuger developed the company until it became a gigantic international enterprise. He obtained monopoly rights in many countries, often in conjunction with the granting of loans. In 1930, for instance, Kreuger made a loan of 300 million marks to Germany and was granted the match monopoly. He soon became a world-famous man, surrounded by mystery and secret international transactions.

When I went to see him he received me in his 'silent room' where it was rumoured that he passed his days in absolute seclusion while dreaming up new and ingenious plans for vast international deals. He greeted me in the old familiar way and asked me to talk about Russia. I did so, and Kreuger put a few questions. It was clear that he was speculating on the possibility of making an arrangement with the Soviet Union on the same lines as he had done with Germany the year before. He accepted my contention that there was hardly any basis for such a deal with Russia, but he added, 'In a few years time we will perhaps be able to discuss this again'.

This was only one year before the collapse of his world-wide financial empire, and his own suicide.

In the autumn of 1931 I was given the task of preparing papers for the forthcoming disarmament conference in Geneva. This was my first experience of that strange and frustrating exercise which is called disarmament.

For Sweden, it was an important conference, particularly as the question of international disarmament was seen in the context of Sweden's own military system. It was no doubt for this reason that the Government appointed a high-level delegation, consisting of three former prime ministers and four or five other political leaders. The oldest member was Mr Hjalmar Hammarskjöld, the father of Dag. At the age of seventy he was intellectually as alert as ever. I travelled with him for two days from Stockholm to Geneva. He was busy writing a study of the flowers of Iceland. As a recreation he read Camoes' *Luciados* in Portuguese. Sometimes he exclaimed: 'This is so beautiful that I will read it aloud to you.' Then he would recite a long passage in Portuguese.

The disarmament conference carried on its debates in Geneva through the whole spring of 1932. It was the largest conference the world had ever seen. Sixty-four countries were represented. We sat in an annexe to the Secretariat, a rather ghostlike building erected by the Swiss Government for the occasion. I don't remember exactly how long the so-called general debate lasted, but in letters to my father I wrote of the monotony of listening to some fifty speeches without simultaneous translation. As few of the speeches contained any new ideas, and had been prepared long in advance with more than an eye on the public opinion in the speaker's own country, it would have been more practical, I said, to have printed all the speeches in a volume to be distributed at the beginning of the conference. The old habitués of Geneva laughed at my childish criticisms. 'Don't you understand,' they said, 'that what is really important is not the speeches but what is discussed confidentially in the corridors of the conference?'

The British delegation proposed the abolition of all 'offensive' weapons, and this proposal, with various additions from other delegations, was made the basis for the further work of the conference to deal separately with Army, Navy, Air and Budget questions. Commissions were set up; new general debates were held and every morning we received a heavy bundle of new papers.

To prohibit 'offensive' weapons is a questionable method of disarmament. I pointed out to the Swedish delegation that the

Lateran Council of 1139 had decreed the prohibition of the cross-bow as a weapon too cruel to be used between Christians. This prohibition had not prevented the armament makers inventing weapons even more cruel than the crossbow.

There were many wise men who shook their heads doubtfully at this vast disarmament conference. Disarmament, they said, cannot be decreed. Only when a state of mutual confidence has been reached can any disarmament be carried out. And then it will come about by itself, without conferences and endless conventions.

But the Charter of the League stated in explicit terms that a process of disarmament had to be accomplished. According to the Treaty of Versailles, Germany and the other defeated states had been made to disarm. The Charter provided for similar disarmament by other states.

There were other arguments in favour of the conference. If Europe, the then centre of the world, was to be led into a period of peace and prosperity it was necessary to stabilize the European political order. Briand had launched the old idea of a united Europe, but this, in the existing circumstances, was obviously a pure Utopian dream. What seemed politically possible, however, was to establish some sort of balance. The heart of the problem was the balance of power between France and Germany.

It was understandable that France would ask for new guarantees of its security as a condition for a reduction of the French forces. It was clear that the German Chancellor Brüning would ask for an increase of German armaments up to a general European level. These were the two given starting points for negotiations. As the United States had withdrawn into distant isolationism, there was only one state which could take the initiative in a high-level effort to find a solution, and that was Great Britain. That was why we all looked forward with excitement to the speech by the British Foreign Minister. That was why his speech was such a disappointment, for Sir John Simon's manner was not that of a statesman but of a successful lawyer. He liked to shine with long *exposés* when, with hand uplifted, he carefully enumerated his arguments. But his conclusions were always deliberately vague, like those of a lawyer when he is aiming not at a judgment by the court but at a settlement out of court. He seemed unwilling to take a firm line on anything.

After the long-prepared aggression by Japan against China, Simon

[73]

declared, 'I am very happy to think that British policy today, whatever may be its short-comings and imperfections, at any rate is a policy which has kept us on terms of perfectly friendly relations with both China and Japan'. The same spirit motivated the British Foreign Minister at the Disarmament Conference.

In spite of this British passivity, there was one fleeting moment in April when it seemed as if a solution was possible. Chancellor Brüning came to Geneva and in the Hotel Metropole, the German headquarters, the chief delegates of the great powers met. It was rumoured that the discussion centred on the idea of an increase of the Reichswehr to 200,000 men, while France should retain an army of 200,000 men in France and 200,000 in the colonies.

I thought that this was the decisive moment of the whole conference. Brüning needed an international success; if he could return to Berlin with a settlement giving Germany the right to double the army he would have a good chance to consolidate his position. France had every reason to help Brüning against the growing threats of the Nazis. An army of 400,000 would give France enough security, particularly with some firm British guarantees.

The discussions in the Hotel Metropole dragged on late into the evening. I stood outside, looking up at the lights in the windows. I waited hour after hour. Then the lights went out one by one. The motor-cars which had been waiting outside the hotel departed and disappeared along the Quai Wilson.

No compromise had been reached. Brüning had to return empty-handed to Berlin.

This was a hard blow for me. I thought the Scandinavian delegations ought to have made representations to the Great Powers. My superiors laughed at my excitement. They called me the impatient Utopian. 'Here we have spent years in preparatory discussions of disarmament. Then you come along expecting the main problem to be solved in three months.'

How many times have I heard officials recommending patience, new deliberations and new delays? Such is the language of those who are considered well-balanced and reliable.

It is, of course, often right, particularly for a small state like Sweden, to be prudent and cautious and to wait. But the greatest of Swedish negotiators, Axel Oxenstierna, knew that there was another side. In his majestic language he declared: 'In all things concerning states and reigns Occasio is supreme.' He knew that particularly in great negotiations it is all-important to seize the right moment for action and decision.

As I sat listening to the long-drawn-out debates I wondered what would have happened if the British delegation had been led by a man capable of taking a long view of the world future, somebody like Lord Salisbury, three times prime minister under Queen Victoria. At least during his younger days he had excelled at making strong decisions in foreign affairs, as, for example, in the Turkish crisis of 1877–8. If the same forceful skill could have been applied to persuading France and Germany at Geneva, a compromise, with some British guarantees, could probably have been achieved.

Salisbury's son, Lord Robert Cecil, inherited something of his father's political far-sightedness. In the early 1920s he spoke of the need to develop the League into a much stronger organization with firm military obligations. He stressed the urgency of the matter. 'I don't believe that we have much time,' he said. 'Perhaps ten years.'

There was another statement that came back to my mind. At the signing of the Treaty of Versailles, Marshal Foch said, 'This is no peace. It is an armistice for twenty years.' Apparently Foch had calculated that the number of men of military age by 1939 would be twice as great in Germany as in France.

It might perhaps be said that these statements made by Robert Cecil and by Foch give the outline of the history of Europe between the two World Wars.

When the Nazis came to power in January 1933, I expected the conference to collapse. But international conferences and institutions often live on although they no longer serve any real purpose.

Surprisingly enough, the Disarmament Conference even had a *seconda primavera*. Anthony Eden, second to Simon in the Foreign Office, was sent to Geneva as temporary leader of the British delegation and I heard from my British friends that the young Minister was full of energy and ideas and that he was determined to take an important initiative. There was much speculation among the diplomats in Geneva as to the nature of such an initiative. I don't think anybody guessed correctly.

[75]

Indeed the British took the most unexpected line, producing a draft of a complete disarmament plan, with detailed figures, for the armed forces of the leading states. The plan was elaborated by Eden and his delegation, but when it was presented, on March 16, 1933, it was the British Prime Minister, Ramsay MacDonald, who made the speech. He was near the end of his long political career and his oratory had become more and more dramatic and bombastic. He shook his white head, he waved his hands and declaimed in his Scots acccent, 'My friends, my friends!'

In spite of MacDonald's unclear and confusing speech, the British plan met with a great deal of response. It seemed as if there was some chance of progress. But one couldn't help thinking of what might have been achieved if a British Foreign Minister had conceived and put forward a similar plan one year earlier, when Brüning was still in power in Germany.

Now it was late; too late.

On October 14 the long-awaited lightning struck. Hitler declared in a speech to the German people that Germany was quitting both the conference and the League of Nations.

I started to pack my bags the same evening, but Mr Sandler,* our new Socialist Foreign Minister, ordered us to stay in Geneva. The conference was not dead, he declared. Negotiations were going on between London and Berlin.

I remained in Geneva until the end of December. Then I returned to the Ministry in Stockholm.

In the autumn of 1934 Anthony Eden came on an official visit to Sweden. In less than two years this young Minister had become established as an international statesman. He had recently been appointed Lord Privy Seal and it was said that his influence with MacDonald and with Baldwin was at least as great as Sir John Simon's.

Eden came to Sweden at Sandler's invitation. The Danish and Norwegian Governments had also invited him so it became a Scandinavian round trip.

I was sent to Malmoe to meet our distinguished visitor, and, as was my habit, I wrote a short description of the trip:

* Richard Sandler (born 1884), one of the leading theoreticians of the Social-Democrat Party. Prime Minister, 1925–6; Foreign Minister, 1933–9.

When I reached Malmoe I called on Papa Fredrik,* who was as friendly as ever, and we walked together to the pier where the boats from Copenhagen arrived. Papa Fredrik, as economical for others as for himself, didn't think we needed a porter; we could very well carry Eden's suitcases ourselves, he said. I replied that it was all right for a secretary like me to carry suitcases through the streets of Malmoe, but not for the Governor of the Province. 'Oh, that's how you see it,' he said, and a porter was engaged.

When the boat arrived, the Governor greeted Eden heartily and we walked to the residence for luncheon. It was all very easy-going and informal. Suddenly a military band struck up in the market-place facing the residence. Eden looked up and I had the impression that he thought the official part of the programme was about to start. But no—it was a company of the Home Guard who had marched up to be inspected by the Governor. He went out and made a short, patriotic speech. When I complimented him on this improvised speech he said smiling, 'But not improvised. As a Governor, I have prepared two speeches. One for the Sixth of November† and one for all other occasions'.

Later, on the train for Stockholm, Eden began to speak of Geneva and the Disarmament Conference. He thought we should all make an effort to keep the conference alive and that Sweden had an active role to play. I mentioned that since I had left Geneva in December 1933 I had been unable to follow the negotiations he had carried on in Paris, Berlin and Rome. Did he think that there was still some chance of an agreement?

Yes, Eden said. During his visit to Berlin in February Hitler had made several concessions: demilitarization of the SS and the SA; arms control; acceptance of France's right to possess heavy arms, etc. Also, the visit to Rome had been a success. Mussolini was clearly interested in an agreement before Germany had gone too far in her rearmament.

The difficulty was really Paris. The French Government had a

* The nickname of Baron Fredrik Ramel. Foreign Minister, 1930–3; Governor of Malmoe in southern Sweden.

† The Sixth of November used to be a great national holiday in Sweden. It is the day when the great King Gustaphus Adolphus won the battle of Lützen in 1632. The king was killed in the battle.

weak parliamentary basis. They hesitated to take decisions. It was understandable that the French were full of distrust of the new régime in Germany, but would it not be better to have an agreement on the limitation of armaments than to have no agreements at all?

This was a question I could hardly be expected to answer. Instead I told Eden something of my own impressions of my visit to Berlin in the summer and my talks with such Germans as Karl Georg Pfleiderer.

Eden listened to me, then asked me if I didn't think that one could place some trust in the Hitler régime.

'Yes,' I said, 'Hitler will keep his promises as long as it is in his interests. But I don't believe he would do so any longer.' Eden agreed that this was quite possibly true, but he added, 'It is in his own interests not to shake the foundations of the whole of Western Europe. This is also the opinion of your Foreign Minister. I believe this is what Sandler intends to discuss with me.'

The following day Sandler had a long conversation with Eden. It must have been a fairly technical discussion as Eden afterwards asked me about some obscure points in the budgetary methods for the limitation of armaments.

The notes I made on Eden's visit at the time end there, but I remember that we went to several art galleries and Eden made a great impression on the experts by his great knowledge of art, both ancient and modern. He carried on a learned discussion on Lucas Cranach, but his real passion was for the French impressionists.

I remember too his telling me about his father, who was rather an eccentric. An agreeable side of his eccentricity, however, was a pronounced taste at an early date for the French impressionist pictures, which then, and particularly in his social circle—the English landed aristocracy—were considered totally absurd. When Sir Timothy died, Anthony Eden was abroad. The trustee was the robust Lord Derby, who was furious when he saw these strange French pictures and ordered them to be sold at any price. 'In that way,' said Eden, 'I lost my only chance ever to possess a collection of French impressionists.'

There were the usual luncheons and dinners. The King gave a luncheon and the British minister, Archibald Clark Kerr, gave a particularly pleasant dinner party. Eden took a special interest in his conversation with Wigforss,* who in his perfect English spoke of the methods by which a government could influence the economic development of a country. Eden told me that similar thoughts were in the forefront of the discussions within the left wing of the British Conservative Party. He considered himself a member of this reformist group, and he mentioned also Oliver Stanley, Walter Elliot and Harold Macmillan.

I found Anthony Eden a very attractive personality and I could not but admire the astonishing rapidity with which, at the age of thirty-seven, he had become an international celebrity. In England he enjoyed the friendship and appreciation of such Conservative leaders as Baldwin and Austen Chamberlain and, at the same time, of the chief critic of the Conservative leadership, Winston Churchill. Within the Labour Party, Eden was better liked than any other Conservative minister at that time. On the international stage it was the same. He had won the friendship and esteem of Doumergue and Barthou, Benes and Titulesco as well as of the Scandinavian Social-Democrats.

The fact that he was very good-looking, particularly well-dressed, and had an aristocratic background, made some people describe him as superficial and even a poseur. This was exactly the opposite of the truth. Eden was, I believe, always a hard-working man. He never tried to compete with Barthou in brilliant conversation. He preferred to listen attentively, an art essential for every diplomat. He had a remarkable gift for establishing good contacts with people totally unlike himself. I saw for myself in Geneva how he could change the atmosphere of a conference from deep pessimism and general distrust to mild optimism and willingness to co-operate.

My real and remaining impression was that Eden was above all an artist. A diplomatic artist.

Unhappily he had the ill-fortune during his first period as a British diplomat to represent a government which had a better chance than any other to guide Europe in a more sensible direction, but which didn't have enough far-sightedness and determination to do so.

* Ernst Wigforss (born 1881), Socialist philosopher and writer. Minister of Finance for twenty years between 1925 and 1949.

VI

Germany

When I left Geneva on being posted back to Stockholm I was assigned to the German desk in the Foreign Ministry, and so for ten years from the beginning of 1934, German affairs were my principal preoccupation.

At this time, and through the remainder of the 1930s, Nazi Germany was the dominant problem in Swedish foreign policy. But it was not only the political aspect, it was also a cultural and moral problem.

It is difficult for young and middle-aged people in the Sweden of the 1970s—and still more difficult for non-Swedes—to realize how deep and intense was the German cultural penetration of Sweden before the First World War. True, this strong German influence was then of relatively recent date. My father's generation retained the French influence which had dominated Sweden since the eighteenth century. As a child, I knew elderly Swedes whose daily conversation was in a mixture of Swedish and French. But from the 1890s onwards it was the winds from Germany which dominated. All Swedes who were at school before or during the First World War learned German before any other foreign language and received an injection of German thought and German culture so strong that it could not but leave its impact for their lifetime.

It was only after the First World War that the winds changed and Sweden came to a large extent under Anglo-Saxon influence.

I can offer my own case as an example of the fundamental German influence on my generation. My parents' house in Stockholm was a centre of music. As I mentioned earlier, my mother was an excellent pianist and delighted in gathering her friends to play in quartets or quintets to which we children could listen from upstairs. What was played were the great German classics: Haydn, Mozart, Beethoven, Schubert, Schumann, Mendelssohn and Brahms. The only non-Germans were Chopin and, very rarely, Tchaikowsky. Music more than anything else gives the atmosphere to a house. My home was steeped in the great music of Germany.

In my school there was one teacher who had a strong influence on me. When he found that I read history on my own he helped me to find books. They were all German. To my teacher, Germany was the only centre for serious historical studies. His models were Harnack, Karl Müller, Otto Scheel and Ernst Throeltsch. He had no contact with the world of Oxford or Cambridge and even less with the Sorbonne. Under his guidance I read a whole library of German history books.

When I was sent on my first journey abroad at the age of fifteen I was terribly nervous as I had never lived with foreigners before. It took me a day and a night to reach the German town of Stralsund. Then I travelled in a noisy little train across the flat countryside of Mecklenberg to Rostock, where I was met by my German host, Professor Reincke-Bloch and his wife. He was professor of history and Rector of the University.

There was still a great scarcity of food in Germany and one ate only cabbage, soup, brown bread and potatoes. (The dear 'Frau Professor' could speak of hardly anything else but food shortage.) My knowledge of German language was strange: I had read so much German historical literature that I could without difficulty carry on a discussion with the professor about Friedrich Barbarossa or the Golden Bull—two of his favourite subjects—yet I did not know the words for the most common objects in the house or in nature.

The University was closed for the summer so I read German literature privately with Doctor Huhnhauser, a heavily-built fat man of thirty who had been an infantry captain in the war. This army experience was a constantly-recurring subject in our conversation when we had finished reading Scherer's history of German Literature. One day I recited Heine's 'The Two Grenadiers' and came to the verse at the end: '*der Kaiser, der Kaiser, gefangen*' ('the Emperor, the Emperor, a prisoner'). Dr Huhnhauser burst into tears. For a second, I was astonished at this emotion over Napoleon —who is the hero of the poem—but then I understood that the emperor who provoked the doctor's tears was Kaiser Wilhelm II, now a prisoner in Holland.

When my teacher had recovered a bit, he began to walk up and

F [81]

down the room. 'We will liberate him,' he shouted in a ringing voice. 'Our day will come. We will kick out this Socialist rabble [*Gesindel*].'

There was somebody else who shared Dr Huhnhauser's opinions. This was Herr Tiedemann, a thin, wiry young lodger in the house. Tiedemann was also a former infantry officer. After the war, he had become a teacher of gymnastics. Hour after hour, Tiedemann trained himself on horizontal bars in the garden. In his pocket he carried a photograph of his wife who was a singer at one of the smaller opera-houses in Southern Germany. She was fair-haired and—to judge from the photograph—at least twice as big as Tiedemann.

'We haven't enough money to live together,' he explained. 'The Socialist rabble who are the government now have dissolved the army. I was dismissed at a day's notice. That is why I have to earn my bread as a gymnast. But our day will come. Then the army will seize power and show the German people their way to the future. We should have won the war. But we were betrayed.'

In those days I had no interest in day-to-day politics but, listening daily to the outpourings of Huhnhauser and Tiedemann, I sometimes put in the mild remark that Professor Reincke-Bloch did not seem to share their opinion. The Professor was a member of the provincial parliament in Schwerin and it was well known that he sometimes voted with the Socialists. The reply was always the same: 'But the Professor is from Southern Germany,' as if that explained everything.

In a spacious upstairs room lived the Professor's mother, a somewhat retiring lady of about seventy-five, who now and then asked me to come up to her room and read aloud. 'It is good for your German and it husbands my eyes,' she said. Her favourite books were German classics—Schiller, Goethe and sometimes Hölderlin. Once, when I came to a favourite poem, she took the book from me and recited the verses from memory. Sometimes the old lady complained about her surroundings. 'I have never felt at home in Northern Germany,' she used to say. 'The people here are very hard.' Then she added: 'Perhaps we have all become hard because of that unhappy war. I often think Germany is losing its soul. It was Prussia and Bismarck who started this misery, although my son doesn't accept that.'

[82]

Her son had been a professor at the University of Strasburg before the war. He was an old friend of Albert Schweitzer, and one weekend Schweitzer came to Rostock. He was then a man of about forty, tall with bushy moustaches and a booming voice. He made a great impression on a boy of fifteen. Schweitzer and Reincke-Bloch soon found their old form as German students. The evening turned into a feast. Instead of the eternal cabbage soup, a juicy steak was put on the table and the Professor produced one bottle of Mosel wine after another. Schweitzer sang students' songs with gusto and our host, usually so serious, laughed until his eyes were filled with tears.

Later Schweitzer told us about his first years in Africa. The worst thing for him had been to be without an organ or a piano. At last he started to play on an ordinary wooden table, while humming the music. He demonstrated this art by 'playing' a fugue by Bach on the dinner table while he hummed the music in his deep bass voice. This was an evening which made my dear Professor very happy.

He needed it, as very soon afterwards he had to face stern tasks. The Coalition government in Schwerin was breaking up and Reincke-Bloch was asked to form a new government. I had to act as a sort of private secretary as there was nobody else to answer the telephone or take an urgent letter. I had my bicycle.

The formation of this new government was quite an event, as it was the first time that non-Socialists had taken over a German provincial government since the war. It was considered important enough for Dr Gustav Stresemann, the leader of the German People's Party, to come to Rostock for discussions with Reincke-Bloch. I went to the railway station to meet Stresemann. Nobody could have looked more like a caricature of a German than he did. His head reminded me of a puff-ball. He did not make a pleasant impression on me, mainly, perhaps, because my dear Professor looked even more worried than usual.

Energetic efforts were now made to form a government on the basis of 'a great Coalition', which meant the participation of all parties from the Social-Democrats on the left to the German National Party on the right. The little parliament in Schwerin, which had—if my memory is correct—sixty-four members, was a sort of comical miniature of the German political scene of the time. I was kept busy bicycling with urgent letters all over Rostock.

The main difficulty was that the leader of the local National Party, a landowner by the name of von Brandenburg, refused to join the Coalition. He was a typical Junker, putting on an air of simplicity and good nature which failed to cover his natural attitude of superiority. '*Ach, mein Lieber*,' he used to say to the Professor and others, patting their shoulders. 'Take care of the government for a while until I can step in at the right moment.' It was whispered that von Brandenburg exchanged letters with the Kaiser in Holland.

Finally, Reincke-Bloch formed a government without the National Party. The evening before the Professor was to present his government to the Parliament, we sat round the dinner table while he read aloud some patriotic extracts of Fichte's *Reden an die Deutsche Nation*. Next day, I sat in the gallery of the rather strange palace in Schwerin where the Parliament met. The new Prime Minister made a long speech, so long that Herr von Brandenburg came close to falling asleep.

Afterwards there was a great deal of photographing. In spite of my Swedish schoolcap, the newspapers presented me as the young son of the new Prime Minister.

This was the first political experience of my life.

During the rest of the summer I took some part in the activities of the young people of Rostock. It was Herr Tiedemann who dragged me along, explaining that there were at least two different groups. *Die Pfadfinder* (boy scouts) were the best, he said. They kept order, marched in organized groups and had a *Führer* (a leader) to direct them. *Die Wandervögel* were much more wild and unorganized. They dressed in a careless and extravagant way and (whispered Tiedemann) some of them were addicted to nudism.

It seemed to me that Tiedemann didn't really like any of the youth movements. Before the war, he said, everybody knew his place. When the time came, one did one's military service for two years and was taught how to behave. After the war, the poor youngsters didn't get any military education, he sighed. How would they grow up if they didn't get together and organize their lives?

Tiedemann and I went with the *Pfadfinder* on long marches in the pine forests on the shores of the Baltic, east of Rostock. We never went on the real *Klotzmarsche*—marches of forty kilometres a day—

but nevertheless, I found our marches more than enough. I wrote a description of one of these excursions to my father:

Yesterday Herr Tiedemann and I travelled all the way to Ribnitz on the Baltic, an old town with walls and towers. We travelled fourth class—standing only and very crowded. We went to a *Feier* (festival) with several hundred boys. In the evening we made a big fire on the shore.

One boy, who is their *Führer*, made a speech about the revival of Germany and how the Reich should be strong again. All the boys were asked to swear on oath that they would give all their efforts to create a new, strong Germany. Then, of course, there was the singing of *Deutschland über alles*. It was all very dramatic, with the sea, the fire and the singing.

I described it to Professor Reincke-Bloch who said he didn't like it; much too pagan, he said, and I think he was right.

In June 1921 I went back to Germany. This second visit turned out to be very different from the first.

I stayed in Berlin with a family called Noack who had a beautiful apartment in Tiergartenstrasse. The father was a professor of classical archeology, but he was travelling in Greece so I never met him. The mother was a lady of great vitality, a sister of the well-known poet, Otto Erich Hartleben. There were two sons. The elder, Moritz, had been through the war and had become something of a mild cynic. He looked upon the intellectual enthusiasms of his mother and younger brother with a degree of scepticism and ironical amusement.

The mother loved to receive the élite of the Berlin academic world and, at that time, the university of Berlin could claim to have an outstanding collection of celebrities.

On the scientific side, there were Planck and Einstein. Einstein, who had just become world-famous, came to tea one afternoon. He seemed at first to be confused and shy, but I believe this was only the way he liked to appear. In fact, I think he rather enjoyed society. His strangely luminous eyes watched the people; as with Moritz, the expression seemed to be one of amused irony.

At the tea-party was a lady in a big black hat who, with great assurance, threw herself into the conversation. She turned to

Einstein, saying that she had, of course, found much of interest in his theory of relativity, but there was one point which she had not understood. How could he claim that the world was without end and still limited? Einstein smiled shyly and then answered: '*Gnädige Frau*, imagine a tennis-ball. On the ball an ant is creeping. The poor little ant can eternally go on creeping round the ball. To the ant the tennis-ball seems without end but in spite of this the ball is limited.' Einstein looked quite pleased with himself and the lady in the big black hat nodded approvingly.

Ulrich, the younger son of the family, kindly gave me a great deal of his time. We walked every morning through the Tiergarten and down the Unter den Linden to the beautiful university building. Ulrich was already working on an historical thesis under the guidance of Friedrich Meinecke and I was allowed to attend one of the seminars of this great historian. It was immensely instructive and impressive to listen to Meinecke analyzing, in a most meticulous and penetrating way, historical documents dealing with the reorganization of the Prussian Army after the Napoleonic War.

But my life in Berlin was by no means entirely academic. Thanks to Ulrich, I saw a great deal of this strange, post-war Berlin, bubbling with the most disparate elements. There was a sense of great release after the long years of grey discipline but there was also great insecurity in daily life and the mounting panic of inflation; there was a problem of unemployment and the threat of the extremist parties of the Left and the Right. Yet there was enormous enthusiasm for all that was new in the arts.

With his magic wand, Max Reinhardt had made Berlin the leading theatrical city of the world. In the summer of 1921 he produced Shakespeare's *Midsummer Night's Dream* in an unforgettable way which to my mind has never been surpassed. He produced Romain Rolland's *Danton* and many other plays. Emil Jannings, Basserman and Alexander Moissi were among the powerful star actors.

Ulrich brought me together with many unusual characters. There was a Dr Otto, librarian in the German patent office, who had formed a club called *Schwimm-Klub geistig hochstehender Herren*. We met in a restaurant near Wannsee. The older gentlemen wore their student-corps caps. There was a bit of swimming before the dinner and a lot of drinking after. Otto was a man full of learning and cynicism. His salary as librarian was far from adequate, but he had succeeded in persuading one of the billionaires of the inflation period —I think his name was Wolff—to make a gigantic collection of books about Napoleon. Dr Otto was for ever telling stories about expensive purchases of books about Napoleon, '*so ein ekelhafter und vulgärer Mensch*'.

Ulrich and I went for a week to a house the family had on Hiddensee, a little island in the Baltic. Ulrich was composing a great tragedy in the Greek style and I was unable to help him. One evening we were invited by Gerhart Hauptmann, who knew the Noack family. Hauptmann was theatrical in every sense. He was very conscious of his literary fame and, equally, of his beautiful head and classical profile. All through the evening he spoke only of his discovery that he was related to Goethe. He had a gigantic plan lying on the floor, showing Goethe in the centre and Gerhart Hauptmann somewhere on the outer edge.

This was the only time I met Hauptmann. Much later I heard that Thomas Mann had drawn a portrait of him as the eccentric Mynheer Pepperkorn, one of the leading characters in *Der Zauberberg*. But there was nothing in the Hauptmann I met that would have made one think of Pepperkorn except, of course, that he was rather affected. Hauptmann spoke clearly, consecutively, and his talk contained no surprises. Possibly he became different after a bottle of Rhine wine or—perhaps more likely—brandy. His nose and cheeks were shining red; more, I thought, than the effect of the Hiddensee sun.

Ulrich had many young friends and, in the evenings, the lively discussions always centred on the present crisis, the future of Germany and the attitudes of the young generation. The intellectual bomb was Spengler's *Des Untergang des Abendlandes*. Many of our friends claimed that Germany should play the role of a Socialist pioneer state according to the ideas of Spengler in his *Preussentum und Sozialismus*. This meant a strict form of national socialism as a means of restoring the Reich to its full power and influence in the world.

Ulrich was violently opposed to these ideas. He was strongly influenced by English historians, particularly by Lord Acton. His doctorate thesis was to be a study of Acton's philosophy of history.

But Ulrich found it sometimes difficult to counter the arguments advanced by the partisans of Spengler. He pleaded for a Germany of the future taking the form of a democracy of the British kind. But did he really believe in this? I don't think so; most young Germans felt that the German state—created by Bismarck with the ensign of the house of Hohenzollern—could only rest on one basis, the German Army.

Some of the young idealists tried to find their *Lebenshaltung* (attitude to life) in a classical ideal against a background of a pessimism inspired by Schopenhauer. A name often mentioned was Otto Braun, and at the Noack's I met Julie Vogelstein, who had just published a book on him. Braun was an infant prodigy who wrote poems in Greek at the age of twelve. Many of his young friends looked on him as a great genius, a young Goethe. He was killed on the Western front in April 1918.

Now, when I re-read the diary and letters of Otto Braun, I have mixed feelings. One cannot but admire the enormous effort of this young man to find a *Lebenshaltung*, but it is in the long run somewhat oppressive when every experience—even the most ordinary—provokes a flood of quotations from the world's literature, beginning with Homer and Dante and Goethe and coming down to Hauptmann and Rilke. But it was in this way that we thought and talked in our circle of friends in Berlin.

After I left Berlin in the autumn of 1921 I kept contact with some of my German friends. We wrote letters and sent books to each other.

During the optimistic latter half of the 1920s I shared the widely held opinion that the German people, thanks to their energy and general ability, would succeed in creating a flourishing economy and that German society would be stabilized by the well-disciplined German workers and by the capable German civil servants and officers.

Keynes' brilliant pamphlet had stirred up violent criticism of the Treaty of Versailles and I shared the opinion that the reparations to be paid by Germany were vastly exaggerated and ought to be revised. But I could not accept the widespread criticism (particularly in Sweden) of the territorial arrangements made at Versailles. I understood the French complaint that France had been left to face a potentially far stronger Germany without having obtained any British or American guarantees. In my optimism, I looked for a

[88]

solution in a rapid strengthening of the League, so as to provide the necessary guarantees.

During my two years in England (1928-9) I always heard expressions of admiration of the German people's abilities and gift for organization. The only criticism to be heard was directed against 'Prussian' officers and Junkers. But—said the English experts on Germany—Prussianism was simply a relic of the Imperial period and therefore of little importance now, compared with the mighty and democratic trade unions.

When, at the elections in September 1930, Hitler's National Socialist Party increased their representation from 12 to 107, this was to many a tremendous surprise. I was in Moscow and saw my friends in the German Embassy every day. I wrote down a short summary of a discussion with Peter Pfeiffer and Karl Georg Pfleiderer:

After dinner I asked Peter what he thought about the election gains made by the Nazis. He said that this was a most serious matter. The programme of the Nazis was a mixture of the most disparate ideas picked up here and there; some socialistic, some nationalistic. The fact that the Nazis had made so many gains meant that there was in Germany a great and increasing number of people revolting against the whole present order of society. Peter hoped and believed that the German Government would strictly carry out its programme without paying any attention to the Nazi gains.

I saw that Karl Georg didn't share Peter's opinions. Before long, he started to talk. He thought that Nazism was an expression of something deeper; the German people were in their hearts longing for a radical change in German society. It was not enough to argue for discipline against the Nazis. Nazism answered many of the deepest instincts and desires of the German people.

Peter replied rather sharply, repeating that the Nazis' programme was a confused mixture of socialistic and nationalistic ideas. What would happen if they were confronted with the hard facts of the real world?

No, said Karl Georg. This whole reasoning is wrong. Nazism is not a programme of a political party. It is a whole new conception of life. Irrational perhaps, but full of life. Karl Georg was now speaking with passion; he was no Nazi himself, he declared, but he

[89]

thought he understood the movement. He would compare the Nazi breakthrough with the advent of Luther, who released an enormously strong revolutionary movement, changing and rejuvenating the whole of Germany and a good deal of the surrounding world.

Weakening Germany and German culture, exclaimed Peter, who, as a good Catholic, was offended by the Protestant Karl Georg's talk of Luther.

I remarked that I never had much sympathy for Luther, whom I always considered to be more of a reactionary than a revolutionary. Was this not also the case with Hitler?

Peter considered Hitler to be a pure demagogue with some primitive basic ideas: hatred of the Jews, agitation against the Treaty of Versailles, etc. Worst of all was his foreign policy 'programme' outlined in *Mein Kampf*. This was a distillation of all the wildest ideas of Pan-Germanism, such as the extension of German *Lebensraum* to include half Russia.

Karl Georg said that he had not read the book, but he had heard from Nazi friends that Hitler had now considerably modified his ideas. It was, after all, a natural process that a movement was launched with a very radical programme which was then modified during the march towards power. The Nazis felt that Germany had a great role to play in Europe. They wanted a strong Germany.

Peter said dryly that there had been other German leaders with the same ideas and this had led to the World War.

Now Karl Georg lost his patience. It was impossible for Germany to remain any longer in the pillory, with unilateral rules for German disarmament. Germany could not accept the Danzig corridor. There must be a new spirit in German foreign policy.

I have quoted this at some length because it is representative o many similar discussions during the autumn of 1930. They revived my memories of Rostock and Berlin eight or nine years earlier. I thought of little Tiedemann in the garden of Professor Reincke-Bloch; I remembered the excursions with the young *Pfadfinder*, their fires, their marching songs and their *Führer*, the debates on Spengler's book and much besides.

I wrote to one of the friends I had made in my time in Berlin. He had always been a Liberal. He answered me in a cautious way. He

GERMANY

spoke of a deep moral crisis and of the need of some sort of 'German revival'.

In 1932 the Nazi Party suffered some reverses. When I left Geneva in December of that year, I decided to stay one day in Berlin. Unfortunately I didn't realize it would be a Sunday. I telephoned my friends but got no answer. I had to spend the day alone, walking the streets. It was a day of restrictions; the restaurants were not allowed to serve a meal until the evening.

I had many happy memories from 1921 and I tried to revive them as I walked from Tiergartenstrasse through the park and along the Unter den Linden, the walk I had done so often with my friends to and from the University. Now, in 1932, the atmosphere was completely different. It was an ice-grey day. People seemed tired and desolate. At last I stopped to contemplate Schluter's equestrian statue of Fredrick Wilhelm. Suddenly I heard a distinguished voice saying in Swedish, 'You are perfectly right. The statue is the only beautiful thing to be seen in the streets of Berlin.' It was my old chief from Paris, Count Ehrensvärd, who, like me, was walking the streets of Berlin waiting for a train.

We dined together. Ehrensvärd said that, unhappily, his gloomy predictions had been proved right. He was convinced that the Nazis would come to power and that Germany would put Europe, and particularly his beloved France, under the threat of war.

Six weeks later—January 30, 1933—Hitler became Chancellor. The Nazis, in hundreds of thousands, marched through Wilhelmstrasse where Hitler greeted them, his arm raised in the Nazi salute. From a window the aged President, von Hindenburg, looked on with the misty eyes of a very old man. 'Where do all those Russian prisoners come from?' he mumbled to his aide.

What could be expected of the new government? This question was discussed endlessly in the corridors of the Disarmament Conference. Some pointed out that the new government included only three Nazis—Hitler, Göring and Frick. All the others were either members of the German National Party or were men without any party allegiance. Most diplomatic observers believed that Hitler must pay great attention to the German National Party, and that he could not contemplate the full realization of the Nazi programme. There was, moreover, the Reichswehr as a guarantee against the more adventurous Nazi ideas.

But in October of the same year, 1933, Hitler declared in a dramatic speech that Germany was leaving both the Disarmament Conference and the League of Nations and he had the full support of the National Party and of the Reichswehr. This decision had the approval of the overwhelming majority of the German people.

I was convinced that this marked the end of the conference, but that was definitely not the opinion of the British or the Scandinavian Governments. They chose to believe that, by negotiation, the conference could be resumed.

In May 1934 I had a short holiday in Dubrovnik. I walked happily in this wonderful old city with its white walls over the Adriatic. Dubrovnik-Ragusa was in those days a little-known holiday resort. There was only one first-class hotel, the old National, with its beautiful garden. When I arrived I found that the greater part of the hotel had been reserved for the chief of the Nazi SA-Troops, Röhm, and some twenty of his henchmen. Röhm was then one of the most powerful men in Germany, commanding more than half a million Brown Shirts. I often saw him in the corridors of the hotel, always in his brown uniform, with a jewel-studded dagger. He was a bizarre figure with his scar-slashed face and his aroma of exotic perfumes. His henchmen were all fair-headed, muscular young men. During the day they lay in the sun in almost total nudity or wrestled on the beach. In the evenings they filled the garden of the hotel, drank copiously of the Dalmatian wines, sang Nazi fighting songs and then sat folded in each others' arms.

This was too much for me. I saw an Italian cargo-boat in the port and asked the skipper if I could embark for Venice.

This was a dream of a journey, exactly as I would always like to travel. A ship without fixed hours. One little port after another; cities with medieval walls and towers; fishermen singing in the early morning; long chats with the crew sitting around a large plate of spaghetti.

I returned to Geneva, but only to say good-bye to the moribund conference. I was then ordered to Berlin for negotiations with Germany. The new leader of German economic policies, Dr Schacht, had introduced a new system for Germany's foreign trade. This was of major importance both for Sweden's large exports to Germany and for the very considerable Swedish holdings of German bonds. The Swedish delegates were Arvid Richert, Björn Prytz and Jacob Wallenberg.*

We were about to leave for Berlin when the world was shattered by the news of June 30, the Night of the Long Knives, when Röhm and his henchmen were shot on Hitler's personal orders and a wave of terror spread across the whole of Germany, with executions of hundreds or perhaps even thousands of people. Was this the beginning of the end for the Nazis, we wondered?

The following day we left for Berlin and two months of intense negotiations leading to a series of agreements for Swedish–German economic relations over the next ten years. But that is another story.

We stayed at the old Kaiserhof Hotel opposite the palace of the Chancellor in the Wilhelmstrasse. Every afternoon an orchestra played in the great hall of the hotel and many people apart from the hotel guests came to take tea or drink a glass of beer. It was mostly a quiet, upper-class clientele. To my utter astonishment one day I saw, sitting round a table, Hitler, Göring and Goebbels. The waiter told me that this trio came every day, or at least every other day. Hitler listened mostly to the music, while Goebbels and Göring talked. As I sat looking at the three of them, the thought struck me that if one could exchange their uniforms for plain clothes they would make a fairly typical group in a German provincial town. Hitler, with his comical little moustache, stretched himself to appear taller than he really was. He might well have been a provincial civil servant, a postmaster or a customs officer; Göring, the butcher of a small town; and Goebbels, the editor of a provincial newspaper.

One evening I attended a mass meeting in the outskirts of Berlin and here was the trio from the hall of the Kaiserhof—but now in a very different setting. Thousands of Nazis, large platforms with mighty swastika banners, batteries of powerful searchlights. Half an hour of exciting marching music and singing in chorus.

Goebbels was the supreme master of mass agitation. But to the Nazi audience the great moment was, of course, when the Führer

---

* Richert I have already mentioned. Jacob Wallenberg (born 1892), Director of Stockholm's Enskilda Bank, 1920–46; President of the Board, 1946–69. The Wallenberg family founded this bank in the mid-nineteenth century and built it into the most powerful group of financial and industrial enterprises in Sweden. Björn Prytz (born 1887), Director of the Swedish ball-bearing company, with world-wide ramifications, 1919–37; Minister in London, 1938–47.

appeared on the platform. For ten minutes they cheered and cheered. I saw people crying with enthusiasm. We soon found the whole scene, and particularly Hitler's staccato voice, so unbearable that we left.

Early one morning in the Kaiserhof my telephone rang. It took me a whole minute before I recognized the voice of Karl Georg Pfleiderer. He avoided giving his name but repeated several times that he wanted to see me. To my surprise, he asked me to meet him in the Zoological Garden. When we met, behind one of the cages for wild animals, I found him very different from his usual self. His round, pink face was unshaven; his clothes were unpressed and stained. He looked around nervously as he spoke to me. He reminded me of our talks in Moscow. He had foreseen the victory of the Nazis and he had greeted with enthusiasm their seizure of power. His friends who had been close to the Nazis were now Party members.

What Karl Georg had wanted, he said, was to make his Nazi friends think in terms of foreign policy. He had been giving lectures to groups of Nazis, and for a while he believed he had acquired a certain influence. But then he had met other groups of Nazis, whom he found very repulsive. They lived only to terrorize; they said their first duty was to liquidate Marxists and Jews. Masses of people were thrown into prison without any legal judgment.

For a long time Karl Georg had tried to tell himself that all these excesses were difficult to avoid in the beginning of a revolution and that the leaders of the movement would soon restore order and discipline. Nevertheless, he had reported some of the misdeeds to the higher authorities of the Party.

The Night of the Long Knives had killed all his illusions. This time it was not a question of excesses committed by a SA Group or small Party officials. It was the Führer himself who had ordered the bloodbath, the campaign of terror and the innumerable arrests. Karl Georg had himself seen the SS police arrest two officials in the Foreign Ministry. Some days ago, a Nazi friend had warned him that his name figured on a list of people to be arrested, probably because he had denounced Nazi actions. He had gone to see the Minister for Foreign Affairs, von Neurath, who, like Karl Georg, came from Württemberg. Neurath said that for the moment he was completely powerless. He advised Karl Georg to keep away from the Ministry until further notice.

I asked him to come to Sweden for a rest. Karl Georg laughed at my simplicity. He would be arrested at the frontier or on the airfield. The only thing to do was to wait until von Neurath was able to settle the matter with the Nazi Party.

I asked what he thought of Hitler's plans for the future. Karl Georg was convinced that Hitler's whole desire was to get more and more power. He had already started an enormous rearmament drive. When he had achieved sufficient military strength he would certainly cancel the main points of the Versailles Treaty one after another: the demilitarization of the Rhineland, the Danzig corridor. One of his dearest dreams was the annexation of Austria.

And then? Would Hitler be satisfied with the unification of all German-speaking peoples from Memel to the Saar, from Sudeten Germany to a revised Danish frontier? No, certainly not. Hitler's programme included war with the Soviet Union and the annexation of the Ukraine.

But, I said, the realization of such a programme must lead to a world war. Hitler, Karl Georg said, is not afraid of war. On the contrary, he is longing for war. But only when he has rearmed.

I knew Karl Georg to be a very emotional man, apt to exaggerate. This time, however, I knew he spoke with bitter moderation and that he was convinced of the truth of his statements. We said good-bye while the wolves in the Zoological Garden started to howl. Karl Georg disappeared into the dusk on his way to one of the suburbs of Berlin where he was in hiding with a friend.

When I returned to Stockholm I was asked to see Mr Sandler, the Foreign Minister, who expressed his thanks for my work on the negotiations in Berlin. I took this opportunity to tell him of my impressions of the Nazis and particularly of my meeting with Pfleiderer. I ended by saying that, however amazing it might seem, it was now a fact that a band of gangsters had seized power in the potentially strongest country in Europe.

Sandler smiled at my outburst. He said that he certainly disliked the Nazis just as much as I did, but it was an exaggeration to speak of the present German Government as a band of gangsters. It was necessary to put emotion aside and look at the situation with a view to reaching practical solutions. The German government must be made to see that unilateral rearmament would arouse the most violent reactions of Western opinion. Germany, openly declaring hostility to the Soviet Union, could not at the same time run the risk of being at enmity with the Western Powers. It was therefore possible that Hitler could be persuaded to accept a general limitation of armaments. Eden's conversation with Hitler in February had shown that the German Chancellor was willing to negotiate.

I said I did not believe in the possibility of sincere German co-operation in the limitation of armaments. On the contrary, what was needed was the rearmament of all Germany's neighbours, including Great Britain and the Scandinavian states.

VII

Darkness over Europe

The rapidly increasing power of a militarized and politically ruthless Germany began to radiate round Europe.

The leading Western Powers, having failed to foresee the massive rearmament of Germany, took no steps to rearm themselves. This could only result in a swift and violent upsetting of the European balance of power.

It was as if a new and powerful magnet had been introduced into a field where the iron filings had long been lying in more or less stable groupings. From 1936 onwards they could be observed spinning around as they sought new positions appropriate to the changed power situation.

Austria was joined to Germany; Hungary began to move closer to Germany in the hope of reversing the Neuilly Treaty; Czechoslovakia looked in despair to France for fulfilment of given guarantees; Romania and Yugoslavia moved gradually, preferring a wait-and-see attitude. Poland, distrusting her alliance with France, pursued an independent policy of direct dealings with Germany.

For some time the small western and northern states pinned their hopes on the League of Nations, thinking that the entry of the Soviet Union could lead to a strengthening of the League. When the decision was taken to oppose Italian aggression against Abyssinia, these countries were in the van, clamouring for the most resolute measures.

I have noted in my diary that two days after the British parliamentary elections in the autumn of 1935 I was asked to see our Foreign Minister, Mr Sandler. He had a number of heavy files on his desk and told me that he was working on a draft Disarmament Convention. He discussed some of the articles and asked me to elaborate some additions. After we had worked an hour or two, I asked him if he really thought it was possible to reach an agreement. Yes, he said. After the British Conservative victory at the elections Eden would certainly press on with his negotiations. Enthusiasm

G   [97]

for the League of Nations had increased tenfold in face of the Italian attack on Abyssinia. If Britain now gave a real lead and Italy was forced to retreat, one could foresee a complete change in the European atmosphere. The Great Powers would reach agreement on a limitation of armaments and Germany would return to the League.

When Sandler said this he was obviously strongly influenced by the wave of optimism in Geneva, caused by the decision to apply sanctions against Italy. All countries, but particularly the small ones, felt they had a tremendous stake in this first serious attempt by the League to stop aggression by the application of sanctions.

But the League's action failed, and the effect on public opinion in the small countries of northern and western Europe was tremendous; even traditionally strong supporters of the League began to waver.

In July 1936 seven states—Denmark, Finland, the Netherlands, Norway, Spain, Sweden and Switzerland—made a joint declaration that the deterioration of the international situation and the resort to force in violation of the Covenant had given rise to doubts as to whether the conditions under which they had assumed their obligations of the Covenant still existed, etc.

In plain words, this declaration meant that, since the leading powers in the League of Nations had not pursued sanctions on a declared aggressor and had allowed Europe to return to a full-scale armaments race, the ex-neutrals had no choice but to return to their traditional policy of neutrality.

There can hardly be any doubt that the majority of the Danes, Dutch, Norwegian and Swedish peoples were happy to go back to neutrality. It was often said that neutrality was not a sure guarantee against war, but that statement could be countered by pointing out that neutrality had, in fact, kept those four countries out of the war of 1914–18.

To some Scandinavians, however, neutrality was not enough. Mr Sandler often spoke to me about the possibility of regional security pacts under the Covenant of the League, and it was clear that he toyed with the idea of a Scandinavian grouping.

This idea is a very old one. To trace its origins one would have to go back to the very beginnings of Scandinavian history, examine the attempts made to create an all-Scandinavian state during the Middle Ages, review the failure of Sweden to bring effective help to Denmark in its fight against German aggression in the 1860s, and take note of the remarkable development of Scandinavian co-operation in most fields of economics, legislation, administration, education and the arts.

Ever since the First World War, the Scandinavian governments had been in the habit of consulting each other on matters of foreign policy. Their ministers met fairly regularly at the League of Nations; indeed at Geneva the Scandinavians felt, and mostly acted as, a close-knit group.

But the optimism of the late 1920s had faded in the disappoint-ments and disasters of the 1930s. In face of the growing menace of Nazism, German rearmament and rapidly increasing military and political power, public opinion in all the Scandinavian countries reacted in very much the same way; with few exceptions the Scandinavians opposed Nazism and particularly its racial ideas, and they deplored the breakdown of the League of Nations, on which they had set such great hopes. These were their reactions; as always the real question was what to do—and the Scandinavian states in 1936 decided on the return to neutrality, although few made any effort to assess the implications of that policy on Scan-dinavian co-operation. Most Scandinavian leaders brushed aside such uncomfortable thoughts.

Mr Sandler was an exception. He tried to face the complications and contradictions which were bound to arise in any confrontation of neutrality with Scandinavianism. This was not an easy task. Sandler became the Hamlet of the Scandinavian drama of the 1930s. He obviously felt that he was a man with a mission, but his mission seemed to take different forms at different times. He liked the epigrammatic style and—not unlike the Prince of Denmark—he preferred the epigrams, which leave the audience puzzled and guessing.

It was not easy to trace and to follow the flight of Sandler's thoughts on Scandinavia; on the rapidly darkening stage of the 1930s he moved about addressing questions and comments—to whom? The Danish Prime Minister, Stauning, had already gone out of his way to attack and condemn any idea of a Scandinavian defensive alliance. This, he declared, was nothing but a dream, and not even a good dream. Even to discuss it could provoke suspicions. He asked Sweden to abstain from interfering in Danish policies.

The Norwegians too were strongly against any plan for a regional alliance.

In Sandler's own Swedish Labour Party the prevailing opinion was certainly that the idea of a Scandinavian defensive alliance was stillborn. Mr Östen Unden, a former Foreign Minister and for decades a leading authority on foreign affairs, warned in no uncertain terms against any such plan.

But Sandler persisted. In the summer of 1937 he made some very pointed comments on the meaning of Swedish neutrality. What were the advocates of neutrality really aiming at, he asked? A Swedish neutrality or a Nordic neutrality? Whatever the answer to this question, Sandler insisted that 'neutrality must never mean that we should accord the same treatment to states who break the international order as to states who keep that order'. Here he was clearly within the basic concepts of the Covenant of the League, namely that there is an international order, which members of the League were obliged to uphold or, at least, not to contravene. A tenacious believer in the League, Sandler was unwilling to give up the defence of its principles or the hope of its recovery.

Moreover, Sandler was certainly—and here he had the backing of the great majority of the Swedish people—inspired by his hatred of Nazi Germany. A leading Swedish Labour paper wrote in March 1938 that 'real Swedish neutrality is impossible in any conflict where Germany is one of the parties'.

This was written only eighteen months before the outbreak of war. But these eighteen months were marked by such headline words as 'Austria joins the Reich', 'Munich', 'The rape of Czechoslovakia', etc., all of which had but one meaning: the ruthless pursuit by the Nazi Government of policies of aggression and conquest while the Western Powers retreated from one line to another.

It was a sign of the times in the late 1930s that the Foreign Ministers of the smaller European states, who traditionally didn't leave their capitals except to go to Geneva, developed a positive passion for visiting other European countries. Sandler was a pacesetter in this kind of travelling. In March 1937 he was invited by Mr Eden, newly appointed Foreign Secretary, to pay a visit to London. I accompanied him.

The first evening Mr Eden gave a banquet at the Foreign Office. In this strange building—said to have been originally designed in nineteenth-century Gothic style but suddenly, on the orders of Lord Palmerston, 'modified' in the direction of a Venetian style— there was even in the 1930s a suite of large rooms used for enter- taining the representatives of foreign countries as in old Lord Salisbury's days. I was both surprised and excited to find myself seated next to Winston Churchill. My other neighbour was Archi- bald Sinclair.

Right from the beginning of the dinner Churchill was in excellent form. I think it amused him to have as his neighbour a very young man quite unknown to him. He directed almost his entire con- versation to me, although he often—and particularly towards the end of dinner—raised his voice so that half of the long table could hear what he said. After dinner several people who had been seated farther away asked me what Churchill had said. I was myself so impressed by what I had heard that I sat down in my room at Claridge's later that night and wrote an account, of which this is part:

Churchill was in splendid form. He didn't drink wine. Every now and then the footman served him a glass of brandy which was rapidly emptied.

He opened the conversation by saying that he was busy writing the history of his ancestor Marlborough and that he had studied the papers dealing with Marlborough's visit to Charles XII of Sweden. 'I don't know if he was a great king,' he said, 'but he certainly was a hero, and this is something more than sheer ability. There was a Swedish minister called Piper who tried to impress Marlborough by keeping him waiting outside his house for half an hour. When Piper eventually came to the gate to receive Marl- borough, the Duke stepped aside to make water—and only then greeted him.'

General laughter.

Churchill: Have you never heard that story before?

I: No, never. Piper probably never told the story to another Swede. But I have read another description of Marlborough's visit —in Trevelyan's book, I believe—and there's nothing there about the encounter with Piper.

Churchill: Certainly not! My old friend Trevelyan is a great historian when it comes to painting broad historical landscapes.

He is so damnably liberal. Everything is progress. Personality and human drama are pushed into the background. But those are exactly the things I will bring into focus in my book. Have you no Swedish books on Charles XII?

I: Yes, there is a whole library. The Swedes never stop writing books on Charles.

Churchill: There you are right. Gustavus and Charles are your two greatest men. But what use have I for your Swedish library on Charles? It's like offering me a treasure on the farther side of the moon.

I: But what sources do you have when writing about Charles?

Churchill: Voltaire, of course! I read him in English and I read him in French. What a writer! I wish I could write like him.

Sinclair: I think you can be quite satisfied with your own style.

Churchill: Satisfied? I tell you, when one is writing a book one is never satisfied. It never turns out to be as good as you would like it to be. But you understand, my young friend, that I write partly to distract me from thinking of our damned British politics.

Sinclair: But you've been extremely active in British politics. Many would say that you have been much too active. (A reference to Churchill's speeches during the Edward VIII abdication crisis.)

Churchill (laughing): To hell with you and your bloody Liberals! This is no time for home affairs. Tremendous things are happening in Europe. Only five years ago we and the French held Europe in our hands. But where are we now? It's Hitler who's sitting at the heart of things in Europe, steadily acquiring more power. I don't know Hitler. He has shown himself to be a master at seizing power. The German people admire him. They always want to have a leader and he has become their Führer. (Churchill pronounced it 'Foorer'.) We've had German leaders before. One was Bismarck, who was a great man. Another was the Kaiser, who was a small man. Both led their people to war. The question is whether Hitler too will lead them to war. We don't know yet. I would like to go to him and say: 'Now you have reached the summit of power. Now you can take your choice. If you wish to become a new Napoleon of war it means that you risk the same catastrophe as Napoleon. But you can also decide to be a Napoleon of peace. Then you can become the central point of Europe, and from Germany can radiate

German energy and German technique all over Europe. It could become a gigantic renaissance in the history of Europe.'

For the last few minutes Churchill had been speaking in such a loud voice that conversation round our half of the table had stopped and everybody was listening; Churchill suddenly fell into silence.

I then said that I didn't believe in a Hitler of peace. I told something of what I had seen in Berlin.

Churchill: If Hitler only wants more and more power and more and more land for Germany it means war. I am prepared for war. But I would prefer to avoid it. My father always told me that we should avoid war with Germany. The Germans are hard, courageous and ruthless. Even if we won it would cost us so much that the victory would look like defeat. My father was right. We won the Great War but what did we not lose? We could not have avoided war in 1914. The question is whether we can avoid it today. That is why I would like to go to Hitler and to speak to him openly and firmly.

I: But the British Government has done nothing else since Hitler seized power in Germany. Sir John Simon went to Berlin only a month after Hitler became Chancellor.

Churchill: Simon is an old woman who can never make up his mind. It is not he who really carries on the discussions with Hitler. It is Anthony. He is young, intelligent and straightforward. Thank God for Anthony! His only drawback is that he is so wrapped up in the League of Nations. He always speaks of articles and resolutions. It's his Liberal blood showing itself.

This discussion was only interrupted by the official speeches, after which Churchill said with a glint in his eyes, 'Well, you realize this means the end of Sweden's neutrality. Now you are on our side.'

I replied that it could possibly have been so if Britain had taken the lead in the League of Nations in the 1920s along the lines recommended by Lord Robert Cecil.

Churchill: The brother of my friend Hugh? You know that the Cecils always believe they are the only ones who really understand the great events in the world. I don't believe that the League, this talking shop, could ever have become a real world organization, a force for peace. But, seriously, what is Sweden going to do to defend itself against Germany?

[103]

I replied that Britain unhappily had abandoned the Baltic through the Anglo-German naval agreement of 1935.

This remark made Churchill burst out in a devastating tirade against the British Government. The guests were now beginning to leave the table. Some turned round to look at Churchill, who with loud voice and raised arm, was addressing a young, unknown man at his side.

I made some hesitant attempts to get up, but Churchill pushed me down. 'Stay here with me,' he said, 'and I will tell you about being a bad Cabinet Minister.' He emptied a glass of brandy, and while the footman cleared the table he spoke at great length and roughly along the following lines: [I began to be a little tired, just as I am tired now, writing it all down.]

'A bad Cabinet Minister,' he said, 'is someone who has imagination. He will often be tempted to speak about what may happen in the future. A British Cabinet doesn't like this. One is expected to be objective. This means that one shouldn't look beyond the current budget year. A bad Cabinet Minister is a man who gives his opinion on the great problems of our time. This, the majority of the Cabinet considers to be high-handed and irresponsible. High-handed because the great problems of our time are not supposed to be discussed in the Cabinet. Irresponsible because there is a risk of causing unrest or grumbling within one or other group in the party. So the greatest of all possible disasters might occur! One might lose votes at the next elections. Cheers for the bad Cabinet Minister!' (Churchill emptied another glass.)

'Tell me about the art of being a good Cabinet Minister,' I said, to fill a moment of silence.

'It is not I who can describe the character of a good Cabinet Minister,' he said. 'But I can show you a few splendid specimens.'

Churchill then stood up, took my hand as if looking for support and we walked through the vast dining-room into the drawing-rooms where all the guests were assembled. Still with his hand in mine, he went straight up to a central table where MacDonald, Runciman and others were sitting. Pointing his finger at them, he said: 'There you have the good Cabinet Ministers.' He slapped my back, turned and went swiftly out of the room.

I felt quite giddy after listening to Churchill's oratory for so long. As I stood there, Alexander Cadogan came up and said with a smile: 'I believe you had an interesting conversation.' 'Yes,' I replied, 'I have never listened to a more dynamic speaker.'

'Yes,' said Cadogan, 'he is really brilliant when it pleases him. What a tragedy that he has now succeeded in putting himself quite outside any possibility of coming back to the Government.'*

The following day we left London for Paris where the French Foreign Minister, Yvon Delbos, gave a luncheon at the Quai d'Orsay. I was fascinated by the brilliant conversation of Leon Blum. I was also intrigued by the new Secretary-General, Alexis Leger. I had heard a great deal about him because there had been tense competition for the succession to Berthelot, who had held the post for almost twenty years and so had been at the centre of French and indeed of European foreign policies. One candidate was Massigli, the leading French diplomat at the League of Nations, a clear-sighted man of strong character. However, he was passed over for Leger, who seemed to be his opposite in many ways. He had dreaming eyes, an olive-skinned face framed by sleek, jet-black hair and the slim hands of an artist. It was said that his melodious voice and unusual gifts of expression had so fascinated the old Briand that he suddenly appointed him Secretary-General of the Quai d'Orsay.

Sandler and I later walked in the Bois de Boulogne and I asked him about his conversation with Eden. He told me that Eden had raised the question of Denmark, asking what Sweden would do if Germany were to demand a revision of the Danish southern frontier. Sandler replied that Swedish opinion was strongly in Denmark's favour, but it would be impossible for Sweden to send troops to defend the Danish frontier.

'Didn't you talk about the Anglo-German naval agreement?' I asked.

'Yes,' Sandler replied, 'I told Eden it showed progress from the point of view of disarmament, but on the other hand it meant a reduced British interest in the Baltic.'

I quoted what Churchill had said to me, that the agreement

* In 1948 I sat next to Mr Churchill at a luncheon in 10 Downing Street. I reminded him of what he had said eleven years earlier. He asked me how I could remember our conversation so well. When I said that I had written it down the same evening, he gave me a friendly grin. 'Before the war there were not many who would want to write down what I happened to say.'

meant that Britain had abandoned the Baltic to its fate and that the
fate could well be Hitler.

I also said that the conversation with Eden had been useful
because we now knew—if we hadn't known before—that Britain was
unwilling to give any guarantees to a possible Scandinavian regional
pact. Sandler denied this. He quoted a speech Eden had made in
his constituency in November 1936 when he declared that there was
a possibility of Britain's military support for any state which had
been attacked.

'Like Abyssinia, for example,' I said.

The following day we flew to Copenhagen, where we had to wait for
the train to Stockholm. We spent the afternoon walking on the
Langelinie, with the beautiful view across the Sound and the
Swedish coastline in the background.

I mentioned that the Danish Prime Minister, Mr Stanning, was
going to London the following week. Would Eden be as reticent
with Stanning as he had been with Sandler? My chief insisted that
Eden hadn't been reticent; he had referred to his speech which kept
open the possibility of British military intervention in support of
any state subjected to aggression. One should proceed step by step.

I said that after some years of studying the Scandinavian situation I had come to a simple conclusion: as neither Denmark nor
Norway would even discuss a Scandinavian defence pact, and
Sweden would probably not wish to enter into such a pact, it would
only be common sense to give up the idea. Instead, the four Scandinavian states should promise each other to maintain a certain
level of military defence. No obligations to assist each other by
military means; only the promise of an agreed minimum of defence.

Sandler showed some interest in this idea, but he felt sure that
the Danes and the Norwegians would refuse an increase of their
armaments to an acceptable level. Then, I said, there was only
one thing to do: Sweden should carry through a rapid and substantial programme for its own rearmament—something similar to
what Switzerland had done. Having rearmed, Sweden would simply
have to sit in its corner and observe the Great Powers' changing
attitudes.

Sandler said that this was a far too simple line to take. We had a
moral duty to co-operate within the League in order to find a solu-

tion to Europe's problems. We shouldn't give up hope of restoring the prestige of the League or of resuming the Disarmament Conference.

But I had heard this many times before; to me these thoughts were unrealistic. I even dared to criticize Sandler's extensive travel programme.* Why go on official visits to Poland and the Baltic states? Wouldn't all this travelling give rise to suspicions and lack of confidence? So the conversation came to an end and Sandler never spoke to me again about the main lines in his foreign policy.

From the time of the Nazi seizure of power in Germany and the collapse of the Disarmament Conference, I was convinced that Sweden ought to return to a neutrality protected by the strongest possible defence system. Already, in Moscow in 1930, Peter Pfeiffer had told me that Hitler's plans must lead to a European war. But in such a war Sweden would be in an extremely precarious position.

It was a fundamental fact that Germany was dependent on imports of Swedish iron ore for her steel industry. The Western Powers would have a vital interest in cutting off these imports to Germany. At the same time Sweden would be heavily dependent on imports from Germany of many kinds of essential goods. The Anglo-German naval agreement had confirmed that Britain had given up the Baltic. Yet the British Government was busily preparing plans for an economic blockade of Germany.

In Sweden we liked to think that the French Army and the British Navy were the two pillars of European security.

In 1938 the Crown Prince of Sweden was invited by President Roosevelt to visit the United States. I accompanied him as his secretary. We saw the President both in the White House and at his country home at Hyde Park. He spoke at great length of the developments in Europe which were clearly a matter of daily worry to him. I found particularly striking his judgment on the West European Powers' military strength. He considered both the strategy of the French and the equipment of their army to be entirely behind the times. He feared that the conservative British Admiralty did not realize the enormous threat which the highly modern German Air Force presented to the British Navy.

* The *Daily Telegraph* wrote that Sandler was the record-holder in the current European competition between visiting Foreign Ministers.

On my return to Europe I went straight to Berlin for new negotiations. This was the moment of supreme crisis in the conflict with Czechoslovakia. I had been given a seat in the Sports Palace where Hitler was going to make an important speech. I sat near Hitler's dais and never will I forget his grotesque, contorted and terrifying face when for an hour and a half he denounced and vilified the Czechs and Benes. The Sports Palace shook with the resounding cheers of tens of thousands of Nazis. There could be no mistaking that the Führer and all his henchmen wanted only one thing— war, and war as soon as possible.

When I returned to the Kaiserhof I found Jacob Wallenberg listening to the radio. I told him what I had seen and heard. 'It must mean war,' I said. 'Hitler wants war—I saw it in his face.' I was excited, naturally, but quite apart from any momentary emotion I was convinced that Hitler really meant to attack Czechoslovakia.

Wallenberg did not doubt this. But, he said calmly, he had telephoned to friends in London and Paris and he had good reason to believe that the British and the French did not intend to fight.

In the spring of 1939 a member of the British Cabinet, Mr Hudson, came to Stockholm. He spoke at great length about the importance of the Swedish exports of iron ore to Germany. If war came, Sweden would prolong it if we did not stop those exports. I pointed out once again that Britain had virtually abandoned the Baltic by the 1935 Naval Agreement with Germany. I knew that Hitler had said, after the signing of that agreement, 'The Baltic is now a bottle which we can close. The British cannot exercise any control there. We are the masters of the Baltic'.

Mr Hudson was accompanied by Mr Ashton-Gwatkin, who was in charge of the preparations for the British economic blockade in the event of war. He told me that the blockade would be of still greater importance than it had been in the last war. The Western Powers were not going to lose millions of men trying to overcome the German fortifications in the West. The next war would be a war in the air and a war of blockade. It would be a prime interest of Britain to hit Germany at one of its most vulnerable points—its need to import iron ore. He understood that a Swedish refusal to export iron ore to Germany would lead to a German attack on

Sweden. But the Swedes should understand that Britain would try 'by all means at her disposal' to stop these exports. He did not believe that the states around the Baltic had any real chance of avoiding being dragged into the war.

In a conversation with a colleague of mine, Mr Ashton-Gwatkin was even more outspoken. He talked of the difficulties the British would have in stopping the transport of iron ore across the Baltic and added, 'I'm afraid we will have to destroy your mines.'

The German officials dealing with Sweden seemed equally pessimistic about our chances of maintaining our neutrality. Ambassador Ritter, who was in charge of German economic foreign policy and at the same time was the representative of the Ministry for Foreign Affairs on the German General Staff, explained many times to me that there would be no place for 'small neutrals' in a coming war. It would be 'a battle between giants', he said. 'The small states will be trampled down.'

Darkness was falling over Europe.

VIII
Autumn 1939

During the fateful autumn of 1939 I kept a diary as usual. Some extracts from it will describe better than any other way what was happening in my life at the time:

September 1: Early to the Ministry. Zenon* comes into my room. He is white in the face and can hardly speak. 'These hounds of hell,' he says at last and repeats it. I too find it difficult to speak, so we stand in silence at the big windows facing the Royal Palace.

'These hounds of hell.' Yes, I understand Zenon's hatred of the Germans, who will now destroy his beloved Poland.

And what about Sweden? Well, after all, we cannot say this is something unexpected. Have we not been waiting for this moment for years?

As I write this late into the night, I am in despair. Could any situation be worse than this? I am not thinking of ourselves. I am wondering if we shall read tomorrow of bombing and destruction in London and Paris?

September 3: Today there is a state of war between Germany and Britain–France. Thank God, I am tempted to say; why didn't we have the war a year ago instead of Munich?

September 4: Long discussion with Sandler. He starts off by saying that in the present situation we have to devote our main attention to the blockade policies. It is essential that the neutrals follow a common line. This ought to be done in two stages. First, consultation between the Oslostates.† Second, consultation between the Scandinavians, including Finland.

* Westrup Zenon Przybyszewski (born 1895), son of the prominent Polish author Stanislaw Przybyszewski. Educated in Sweden and became a Swedish citizen; Minister in Berne, 1940–6.

† Oslostates: The Scandinavian countries, the Netherlands, Belgium and Luxembourg.

I said that the most important thing is that Sweden should soon start negotiations with Britain. Come to an agreement with the British, then tackle the Germans—we must do the opposite of what we did in the First World War.

Sandler approved of this. But we should not do it alone; only in conjunction with all the neutrals, etc.

What can we do now? The Oslo group can hardly give us anything. The Scandinavian group perhaps. Although I doubt it after my experiences with them in the last few years. As to Denmark, it seems quite clear to me that the Danes give first and absolute priority to Germany. This Sandler will not believe.

The British Minister delivers a memorandum on the coming British blockade—an elaborate document mainly on the lines one expected. Long internal discussion with Sandler and Boheman. I am asked to draft an answer. We are all agreed that we ought to reply promptly.

In the evening I sit writing in the Ministry. Sandler telephones . . . He makes a few amendments to my draft, then says we can hand over this memorandum to the British Minister.

September 8: The British Minister came to see Boheman. I was present. The Minister is best described by his own name: Sir Edmund St John Debonnaire John Monson (Baronet). It is not Wodehouse. It is much better, and genuine.

Erik Boheman * gave, in my opinion, a really brilliant exposé of the Swedish policy of neutrality, our desire to negotiate first with Britain, etc. Monson seemed to listen attentively but he made no notes. Boheman concluded by handing Monson our memorandum. Monson then explained with much stuttering that his cipher didn't function very well. Could we not transmit our memorandum through our Minister in London?

What an anti-climax!

We have a long discussion about the composition of the delegation to London. It is clear that the leader should be Boheman, who knows both the political and the economic side . . .

Two heavy Norwegian tankers fully loaded with oil came sailing

* Erik Boheman (born 1895). Secretary-General, Swedish Foreign Office, 1938–45; Minister in Paris, 1945–7; Ambassador in London, 1947–8; Ambassador in Washington, 1948–58.

along the western coast of Sweden on their way to Hamburg and were stupid enough to enter the Swedish port of Helsingborg. The Customs telephoned asking how the newly-issued prohibition on exporting oil should be applied. When the question was referred to me my first thought was how important it was for us to inspire confidence in the British. We are, after all, entirely dependent on them for our own urgent needs of oil. I asked the Customs to detain the two tankers. The Swedish Navy had to intervene. The Minister of Defence called a meeting. It was amusing to see how his warlike instincts rapidly came into play. 'Would you like me to send a destroyer to protect the entrance to the port,' he asked. When I said 'Yes' he seemed delighted.

September 15: The British ask for negotiations very soon—precisely what we would like ourselves. But Boheman can't leave for London before the meeting of Scandinavian Prime Ministers and Foreign Ministers in Copenhagen on September 18-19.

September 20: I write after my return from Copenhagen. We had two days of uninterrupted discussions about the coming negotiations with Britain and Germany, but I didn't find them very rewarding. It is really a mistake when Foreign Ministers play the role of experts.

The Danish Foreign Minister, Munch,* gave a reception. There were hundreds of people. These Scandinavian mass meetings make me nervous. There is such a contrast between the façade and the inside content. I suffered for a while, then decided I could slip away. I went back to the Hotel d'Angleterre and sat down on the terrace with a bottle of beer; very pleasant after all the noise and chatter at the party.

Suddenly I saw a heavyweight figure crossing the road, hat in hand. It was Per Albin Hansson. He came straight to my table and sat down heavily.

'So you slipped away,' he said with a grin.

'Yes,' I said,—'I found it all rather gloomy. The gloomiest is always Munch himself. I've now met him so often here and in Geneva that I think I know him well enough.'

* Peder Munch (1870–1948). Danish Liberal leader; Minister of Defence, 1913–20; Foreign Minister, 1929–40.

'You know, I'm not much impressed by all this Scandinavian talk,' Per Albin said. 'I don't think Stauning [the Danish Prime Minister] will change Danish policy in the slightest degree to bring it into line with the other Scandinavian countries. But it has been good to get away from the pressures of Stockholm for a couple of days. Since the war began, I haven't had a chance to sit down and think. But here in Copenhagen, when they've been debating all sorts of things, I have been able to sit back and think.'

He was silent while he emptied his first bottle of Carlsberg.

'You and Boheman have often said we were heading for a new World War, but I must say I never thought the people who went through the first war would ever let themselves be dragged into a new misery.'

'But Mussolini and Hitler have been preaching the gospel of war for years now,' I replied.

'Yes, but this is precisely what shakes me most,' Per Albin said. 'The first war was started by emperors, Tsars and European capitalists, but both Hitler and Mussolini come from the working classes. How can they want war, which will cause the working classes unlimited sufferings? Isn't it damnable that everything I and my comrades in the Party have worked for will now be ruined?'

September 22: There is something particularly sinister about the Russian occupation of Eastern Poland. I say sinister because that is the word to describe the interplay between the two deadly enemies, Nazi Germany and the Soviet Union.

I must add that I understand Moscow's policy up to a point. The unfortunate Conservative Government in Britain has given the impression of wanting to come to an arrangement with Hitler, although they must have known that Hitler would then attack Russia. It is certain that's how Stalin has interpreted Chamberlain and Munich. It was probably then that he took the decision to make a *renversement des alliances.*

Has British foreign policy ever been so mishandled? Munich was a staggering mistake. Later, when the decision was taken to change the policy, another major mistake was made. Britain gave guarantees to Poland before trying to come to an agreement with Moscow. Once the guarantee was given to Poland, Moscow could be sure that

Britain would be at war with Germany before Hitler could attack Russia.

October 3: Sandler tells me that whereas he has believed until now that our main problem would be the blockade as in the first war, now he fears that the problems of pure power politics will be dominant. It becomes clearer every day, he said, that the Soviet Union, after the pact with Germany, is moving forward on the eastern shores of the Baltic. He feared that Russia would make claims to Finland.

I maintained my long-held opinion that neither the old Tsarist Russia nor the Soviet Union had any desire to conquer Scandinavia. The question of the security of Leningrad was quite another matter. Anybody travelling from Helsinki to Leningrad could see how close the frontier was to the very gates of Leningrad.

Sandler listened with an enigmatic smile. He asked me to draw my conclusions. 'I believe the Finns ought to negotiate,' I answered.

'That is exactly what I believe they will have to do,' he replied.

October 12: Today something unbelievable happened. I was sitting with an Estonian delegation. Our negotiations have become more and more nebulous as the whole future of Estonia is so uncertain. My telephone rings. I hear the voice of the Prime Minister. He wants me to come at once. I have to excuse myself, saying that I am in a meeting with a foreign delegation. He grumbles a bit.

But when I went to see him he was, as always, most friendly. Then he explained that he was making some changes in the Government. One seat would be free. He wanted to find somebody who knew the Swedish economy and had real knowledge of foreign policy. He had thought of me. As soon as he had said this he laughed; I looked so astonished, he said.

'Yes,' I said, 'I couldn't be more astonished if you had asked me to be a bishop.'

This amused him greatly. 'Well, when the right moment comes, perhaps I'll speak to the Minister for the Church about that!'

In a more serious vein, I said that I had never belonged to any political party, although I had twice voted Conservative.

'How can an intelligent man—as you are—vote Conservative?' he asked.

'To give a chance to the parties in the middle.'

'Yes, that might be a valid reason. But, frankly, it is of no importance that you have voted for this or that party. We need you in the Government. You can give me your answer tomorrow.'

I left the Prime Minister's office somewhat perturbed.

The intention seems to be that my real work will be the negotiations with the belligerents. I must have an assurance that I will retain control of my department in the Ministry of Foreign Affairs.

October 13: Told P.M. that I am ready to enter the Government. I am happy that Chamberlain has turned down Hitler's 'peace' offer so decidedly.

October 14: Sworn in as a Minister. The King and the Crown Prince were present.

October 15: Early in the morning I was called to a meeting with the full Government. Sandler put forward proposals for the laying out of a minefield at the Aaland Islands. Immediate opposition from Mr Wigforss (Minister of Finance). Soon the discussion broadened to include the whole of our policy towards Finland.

I was, of course, silent. A minister for only twenty-four hours!

After the meeting I walked back with K. G. Westman (Minister of Justice—a former Minister for Foreign Affairs). He said that Sandler was too wrapped up in the ideology of the League of Nations. He still believed that one could stop such wild animals as Hitler or Stalin by resolutions adopted by the League or by the reactions of world opinion.

October 16: In the morning the P.M. spoke to me about the forthcoming meeting of the Scandinavian Heads of State. It is Sandler's idea, he said. For himself, he looked forward to this meeting with mixed feelings.

I said that it would be better for the Finns to try to negotiate privately in Moscow. All the protests and publicity in the world press must leave Moscow totally indifferent. Having made a pact with Hitler, Stalin certainly does not care a damn about Western public opinion.

October 21: After the meeting of the Scandinavian Heads of State,

Svenska Dagbladet writes: 'No possible doubt about the firm attitude of the northern countries.'

Le Temps in Paris declares that now 'a real Northern bloc' has been formed. It is not the fault of the newspapers. It is the whole theatrical staging of this meeting between three kings and one president which has given so many people, both in Sweden and in Finland, the false impression that something has really happened during the meeting.

October 22 : A more than dramatic government meeting. Sandler gave a long account of the question of laying minefields in the Aaland Islands and Wigforss broadened the debate to encompass our whole relationship with Finland. Then Sandler made a personal statement. The Government disapproved of his plan for the defence of the Aaland Islands; this meant that the Government disapproved of a main point of his foreign policy. He was quite clear about the consequences to his personal position. But there was another matter. To have a ministerial crisis now would be impossible in view of the current negotiations between Finland and Russia. When that situation was clarified it would be time enough to reopen the personal question.

Now Wigforss spoke. He had no wish to push the Government in a direction in which it didn't really want to go, but he had, of course, his own convictions and his own responsibility. He was no pacifist in the sense that he thought that one should never fight. But if we were obliged to fight we should fight for Swedish interests. It had been said that he ought to have made clear earlier his doubts about the wisdom of the foreign policy with regard to Finland. If he now seemed to have hardened his opposition it was because we had reached a decisive point; he was quite prepared to leave the Government.

He was interrupted by Sköld (the Minister of Defence)* who declared that as it was clear that the Government was divided, Sandler and Sköld should resign and Wigforss ought to form a 'pacifist government'. When Wigforss shook his head, Sköld interjected, 'You can't be such a damned coward! You have to face the consequences'.

* Per Edvin Sköld was Minister of Defence, 1938–45. He has also been Minister of Commerce, Agriculture and Finance.

The P.M. made a great effort to sum up. A ministerial crisis would mean the breaking up of the present parliamentary system. If everybody insisted on his own opinions without considering the need of co-operation within the Government, then not only the personal but also the political consequences must be faced. He would be quite willing to give up his post as Prime Minister. Somebody else—for instance, Wigforss—could take over. This worried him less than the breaking up of the parliamentary basis of the Government.

October 27: I had a long discussion with Wigforss regarding our negotiations with Germany, particularly the exports of iron ore. He agreed with my proposals. He has invented a curious system of indicating, by small movements of his head, his agreement, disagreement or doubts. He is an unusual type. Pacifist, teetotaller, radical, but above all an intellectual with a strong taste for power, and therefore to an unexpected degree a realist. He is undoubtedly the most remarkable man in the Government, but I don't think he would be the right man as head of the Government.

In the afternoon Jacob Wallenberg and I discuss the negotiations with Germany. The dominating problem will, of course, be the iron ore. The Germans will claim unlimited Swedish exports. The British have adopted the 1938 figures as normal. This would mean some 10 million tons of ore. But can we go that far? We must await more detailed reports from Boheman and Marcus Wallenberg in London.

Jacob Wallenberg repeats that he entirely accepts that we must first try to come to a general agreement with the British, and then negotiate with the Germans. But he also repeats what is so typical of his character!—that 'we must be clear in our minds as to where we stand'. He questions whether the Government understands the real situation in Europe. Germany has a crushing military superiority over the Western Powers. It is easy to say that we should stake all on a British victory, but the real question is how shall we manage in the next few years without falling under German domination?

I say that it seems that many people in London hope for an internal collapse in Germany. Jacob, who has excellent contacts with various groups in Germany, replies that there is no chance of such a collapse unless Hitler suffers a great military reverse. Before Munich there had been a chance. Not now.

I sit tonight thinking of what Jacob said. I am convinced he is right. Germany has a great military superiority. Even if France and Britain can hold the Western Front long enough to have time to rearm, I can't understand how they will ever be strong enough to break down Nazi Germany. During the First World War they had Russia on their side. When Russia collapsed, the United States came to the rescue. Without this, they would never have won the war. This is what people forget.

October 28: Sitting on the ministerial bench in Parliament, I was surprised by an attack on the Government's attempt to reach an agreement with France. At last there was nothing else to do but make a speech, although I know, of course, that an extra-parliamentary Minister is not really supposed to speak. When I said 'Mr Speaker' all nervousness disappeared and I had the strange feeling of speaking in an airless room, although I could see with my physical eyes some hundred members of parliament around me. When I finished and sat down I was as calm as ever. Now I have reflected on this—and will probably be nervous next time.

October 30: The Prime Minister came into my room to congratulate me on my maiden speech. I was surprised and touched. How could he find time to think of such a small matter? But he was quite serious about it. He spoke about his own first steps as a parliamentarian, about the art of composing a speech, etc. He ended by saying that he felt that I ought to enter upon a political career, adding, 'Of course you must choose the right party!'

October 31: Boheman, on his return from London, makes a report to the Government. He considers—rightly—that he has had a success beyond our expectations. To have persuaded the British to accept 'normal' exports of iron ore to Germany is something we had always hoped for but never really believed in.

I said that I simply couldn't understand the British having been so reasonable. He explains that the British attach the greatest importance to fixing a maximum limit. They don't believe in a long war. They consider that the German military superiority is being reduced day by day. They claim that the Western Powers will have superiority in the air some time next year.

It seems almost as if Boheman shared this extremely optimistic opinion. My impressions are mostly based on German sources and I am of an entirely opposite opinion.

November 5: It is now decided that the British Minister, Sir Edmund Monson, will leave Stockholm. This is probably a good thing for Sweden. His successor is called Mallet. He has been first Counsellor in Washington, which probably is a sign that the Foreign Office considers him to be very capable.

November 14: The Swedish–German negotiations have broken down.

November 19: A French paper calls Hitler 'a hesitating Hamlet'. This is certainly the most misleading assessment ever made.

November 20: Sandler says that the general atmosphere in Finland is now rather optimistic. People who left Helsinki in October are moving back. The Finnish Foreign Minister still seems to assume that the Russians are bluffing. Sandler doesn't share this opinion any longer. He avoids answering questions.

November 28: Russia denounces the non-aggression pact with Finland. We are moving towards war.

November 30: Russia attacks Finland. Helsinki is bombed. The P.M. comes to my room saying that he will now try to form a government based on a broad coalition.

He asks me what I think of Germany's attitude. I said that it seemed quite clear that Germany approved of the Russian action. I thought that the Germans didn't wish an intervention by Sweden because this might lead the Western Powers to intervene. The exports of iron ore could be endangered.

December 3: The war in Europe is certainly becoming more and more threatening to us. As for myself, I am longing to go back to my real job—negotiations with the belligerents. I find it frustrating to sit in the Government, cut off from my real field.

December 4: The P.M. came early into my room and said he had now definitely decided to form a broad coalition government. The world situation made this necessary.

I see that the German newspapers attack Sandler for having 'compromised the traditionally good German–Swedish relations'. Yes, we have all known that Sandler had become *persona non grata* in Berlin, but I had not expected the Germans to interfere so clumsily in the formation of a Swedish Government.

December 13: Change of government. We who are leaving the Government were in city dress when we went to the royal palace to make our bow to the king. On the staircase we met all the new ministers, in white tie and with decorations.

It has been a short period for me as a Minister. When I was appointed the newspapers claimed that I was the youngest minister in modern Swedish history. I don't think this was right. But today I can claim a record. It has certainly never happened before that just before his thirty-fifth birthday a Swede can call himself *ancien ministre.*

December 16: I am leaving for Berlin. My mission is rather peculiar. The new Commander-in-chief, General Thörnell, has made out a list of armaments—artillery, tanks, aeroplanes, etc. The total value is 500 million crowns. The Swedish defence staff believes that Göring would be prepared to deliver all this to Sweden to strengthen our attitude towards the Soviet Union.

In and around the staff there is much loose talk about Göring and his presumed sympathies with Sweden. But I ask myself, is it not rather fantastic to believe that Germany, preparing herself for a gigantic offensive in the West, would be willing to deliver war material in such quantities?

Handing me his list, the General looked sternly at me. It is of decisive importance, he said, that the arms be delivered before April. I suppose this means that the military staffs are counting on the possibility—probability?—of Sweden being involved in war in the East before the end of the Spring.

December 23: My mission was unsuccessful—as I expected. The Germans smiled at our list. 'We are fighting a war. We need all our arms ourselves,' they said.

As far as I can see, Germany is giving full diplomatic support to Moscow in the war against Finland. How can we imagine that the German Government would be willing to send masses of arms to Sweden while we are fully occupied sending arms to Finland?

December 28: We publish a little notice in the newspapers that we have made an agreement with Britain. A few days ago we signed an agreement with Germany. We have succeeded in our double negotiation. In the First World War we reached this result only at the very end. This time we have succeeded after less than four months.

There is nobody outside the Goverment and the little group of negotiators who pays any attention to this positive result. Public opinion is, of course, entirely absorbed by the Finnish–Russian conflict.

December 29: The German Foreign Ministry's periodical *Deutsche Diplomatpolitische Korrespondenz* declares with great emphasis that if Sweden relaxes her neutrality Scandinavia will be dragged into the war. This, they claim, is the aim of the Western Powers.

It is now decided that I shall go with Prince Bertil* to Washington in order to persuade President Roosevelt to give his agreement to American deliveries of arms to Sweden. I am happy to do this. I am very attached to the Prince. I long to gain some insight into the only country capable of helping the West to win the war.

January 1, 1940: Last night I listened to a radio speech made by our new Foreign Minister, Mr Günther.† He said, 'This New Year's Eve it is as though we are facing not only a new year. It is as though our whole past life had come to the end of a period, and we were now emerging into something new and uncertain.'

Yes and no. Certainly I realize that all values are now in the balance, but the essential is, after all, that we are prepared to defend *our* values.

* Prince Bertil of Sweden (born 1912), third son of King Gustaf Adolf VI.
† Christian Günther (born 1886). Entered Foreign Office 1925; Permanent Under-Secretary, 1934–7; envoy in Oslo, 1937–9; Foreign Minister, 1939–45.

PART TWO

PART TWO

IX

Westwards

It was cold and depressing in Stockholm in January 1940. The icy winds from Siberia had broken through to the shores of the Baltic and at the same time the Russian armies were making new attacks on Finland. The war in Finland occupied all our minds and deep anxiety was the prevailing mood.

In our new Coalition Government there were deep divergences between the 'activists' and the partisans of a cautious policy with the Prime Minister, Per Albin Hansson, trying to mediate between them. He told me he was convinced that the great majority of the Swedish people wanted to give substantial aid to Finland but not in such a way that Sweden would be dragged into the war. He saw himself as the spokesman for this opinion.

Some well-informed people had heard that I was against the activist agitation.

When I was accused of being 'anti-activist' I always answered that I was in favour of substantial aid to Finland but a Swedish intervention in the war would in all probability lead to manoeuvres by the Western Powers in north Scandinavia and a German *riposte* would then be a certainty. Moreover, I always suspected that Hitler wanted to use the Russian-Finnish conflict to put the Western Powers in open conflict with the Soviet Union.

I was fully occupied with preparations for the journey to Washington. I was given endless lists of war materials to be bought in the United States and I was instructed to persuade the American Government to grant Sweden a substantial loan in dollars.

A few days before our departure Prince Bertil and I were asked to come to a meeting with the Minister of Defence. The spokesman of the Swedish Navy, Admiral Tamm, declared that it was essential to improve our naval position by the acquisition of a fairly heavy cruiser. The Minister of Defence turned to Prince Bertil and me, saying that the only country able to sell us a heavy cruiser was the

United States. I pointed out that it wasn't the President but the Congress who was competent to authorize the sale of war material and it seemed unlikely that the Congress, with its isolationalist majority, would like to see a heavy cruiser sent to the Baltic. The Minister looked sternly at me; obstacles, he said, existed in order to be overcome.

Before leaving I had a long talk with the new Foreign Minister, Mr Günther. I quote what I wrote down after the conversation:

Günther agreed entirely with my long-held opinion that it was wrong to try to impress Stalin by Western propaganda or diplomatic representations in Moscow. The right method was secret negotiation between Finnish and Russian leaders. He said he intended to try to pave the way for such negotiations.

When I spoke of my fears of the announced intervention by the Western Powers in Norwegian waters, Günther replied that he was just as worried as I. I wondered if we shouldn't draw the attention of President Roosevelt to the likely consequences of a British intervention.

Günther thought that London would take it very much amiss if we tried to 'mobilize' Washington. But, I pointed out, we had 'mobilized' Washington several times in order to persuade the Americans to plead the cause of Finland in Moscow. We did this although we ought to have known that after the Russian–German pact Stalin wouldn't care a damn about Western opinion. On the other hand it was absolutely certain that London would have to pay attention to an opinion expressed by Roosevelt.

Günther said that he would think it over.

We travelled by train to Genoa, to embark on the American liner *Manhattan*. It was strange to be standing on the upper deck in clear Mediterranean sunshine after so many months of incessant work in Stockholm ministries. The change was too violent. The doctor declared that I was overtired and that I needed some days of rest, so I had to take to my bed.

But the difficulty was to keep my thoughts under control. My mind always turned in the same circle: Finland—the British threat to the Norwegian coast—the near certainty of an immediate German intervention. Jacob Wallenberg had told me that one of his German friends had dropped him a hint about the German staff discussing military action against Norway.

Hoping to get away from these thoughts, I began to read the diary I had kept in the summer of 1938 when, as secretary to the Crown Prince of Sweden, I had made a two-month visit to the United States—my first experience of America. Only eighteen months had passed since then yet how vastly the world had changed! And how different the mood of that pre-war journey. For example:

June 17, 1938: The Crown Prince telephoned from Gothenburg to speak to his father, who had taken such an active part in yesterday's festivities on his eightieth birthday. The news was that the old boy had been playing tennis!

June 19: The *Kungsholm* (Swedish Atlantic liner) carries a strange cargo: one Crown Prince, one Crown Princess, one royal Prince, two Ministers of the Crown, two bishops, two governors, not to speak of industrialists and male voice choirs. Who had this fantastic idea of sending a shipload of Swedish dignitaries across the Atlantic to celebrate the Tercentenary of some small Swedish settlements on the American coast? But it is fun. Perhaps even sensible. As European affairs seem to go steadily from bad to worse there is every reason to cultivate our relations with North America.

June 27: It is raining. We arrive at the quayside in Wilmington, Delaware, dripping wet. On the top of a towerlike platform President Roosevelt is standing in the middle of a forest of top-hats and umbrellas.

In the evening, dinner with Henry du Pont, then a party at Pierre du Pont's for at least a thousand guests. My neighbour at dinner spoke incessantly of the family du Pont, who—it seems—own practically the whole state of Delaware. My talkative neighbour said that it was a sensation to see the President—'this red Radical'—on so intimate terms with the du Ponts, who are, of course, the very essence of American capitalism. The President and Prince Bertil have great fun together.

July 13: In Detroit. Old Henry Ford invited Prince Bertil to breakfast and was delighted when he discovered that the Prince is a real expert on motor-car engines. He showed his designs for the first (the classical) Ford car. 'I had very little money,' he said. 'Everything I could earn was spent on the construction of my first model. I had my meals in an inn and when I couldn't pay my weekly bill I told the proprietor I would pay him in shares in my future company. He replied that he wasn't mad. Well, if he had been, he'd be a multi-millionaire today,' Ford laughed.

President Roosevelt fascinated me. We met him not only in Delaware but also in Washington and on his estate, Hyde Park. His enormous personal charm, making anybody feel at ease, was well known, but what fascinated me particularly was his curious mixture of far-sighted statesmanship and intense interest in the smallest details of American home politics. He told the Crown Prince (and remember this is July 1938) that he considered the strategical concepts of the French military leaders to be as much behind the times as the French military equipment. He thought that the British Navy didn't realize the immensity of the threat of the German Air Force. At the same time, he could spend hours telling stories about American politicians and their manoeuvres.

My pessimism about the prospects in Europe convinced me that the only hope for Western civilization was the United States.

To return to my 1940 journey, I was able, after a few days in bed, to join the others on deck and we worked assiduously to prepare ourselves for our task in Washington.

In describing our six weeks in Washington I shall turn to the account I wrote almost immediately afterwards. On the return journey to Europe we were stranded for five days in Bermuda and two days in the Azores—such were the travel conditions of the time on the only airline across the Atlantic—so I passed the waiting days by writing:

On the outward journey Admiral Wijkmark was always reminding us of the cruiser. I listened patiently but never made any comment. I was unable to treat the question seriously.

In Washington and New York people seem eager to ignore the happenings in Europe. In fact the news of the war is relegated to the back pages of the newspapers. Speaking to businessmen, one has the impression that their attitude to Europe is governed by a determination never to be dragged into the war. Yet there is enthusiasm for Finland and the heroism of the Finnish Army. On the other hand, the Americans often make indignant criticisms of Sweden's passive, even 'cowardly', policy. (It is amusing that in making this criticism they never seem to reflect on the passivity of their own country—potentially the most powerful state in the world —with regard to Western Europe.)

I was, of course, prepared to find American public opinion dominated by the isolationist ideology. But I must say that the isolationism is even more pronounced than I had imagined.

It is, no doubt, easy to understand that when people in England and France insist on speaking of 'the phoney war' (or *la drôle de guerre*) the Americans on the other side of the Atlantic find it difficult to take the war really seriously. In New York I heard a limerick aimed at Neville Chamberlain:

> *An elderly statesman with gout*
> *When asked what the war was about*
> *Replied with a sigh*
> *My colleagues and I*
> *Are doing our best to find out.*

On the question of a dollar loan I turned first to the Export and Import Bank. I was then told that it was the head of the Reconstruction Finance Corporation who was competent to approve or disapprove requests for credits from foreign buyers. The head is Mr Jesse Jones, a multi-millionaire from Houston, Texas. He is certainly one of the most difficult men in Washington to contact, but our Minister knows him (they play poker together) and when he telephoned we were immediately given an appointment.

Jesse Jones received us with all the expansive hospitality of an important man from Texas. He showed us a gigantic model of the city of Houston which seems to be his favourite toy. After a few jokes about the last poker game, Jones settled his tall frame in his chair and putting his feet on his big desk, said, 'Well, young man, get going, if you please.'

I explained Sweden's dollar situation and gave him some facts

I   [129]

about the Swedish economy, our need to rearm in the present situation in Europe. I knew this speech almost by heart, but it was difficult to concentrate as Jones had the intimidating habit of spitting right across the desk in the direction of a spitoon about a yard away. He always hit the target. After about half an hour Jones suddenly said, 'That's enough. I'm with you. Let us have another meeting on Thursday.'

On our way out I told Jones that we were anxious that our demand for a loan should be kept a strict secret. 'Trust me, my boy,' he assured me, slapping my back.

On Thursday morning we presented ourselves again. Jesse Jones received us with his long legs again resting on his impressive desk. In a corner of the room two men were seated. They were not introduced. Jones whispered to me, 'Repeat what you said last time, but in a loud voice so that the men in the corner can hear you.' Somewhat mystified, I repeated my report. Jones sat up in his chair and said with, for him, unusual formality, 'Well, we will have to consider this very carefully.' The two men then left the room.

When the door closed, Jones broke out in loud laughter. 'Those were newspapermen,' he said.

'But we agreed not to have any publicity,' I protested.

'Yes, that's exactly why I asked the newspapermen to come. They have been allowed to listen to your report, but only under promise of secrecy. If I hadn't invited them, there would have been considerable risk of their making conjectures about your visits to me. Now they are bound by their promise.'

Then Jones said that we didn't need to have any more meetings. He would that very day authorize the Export and Import Bank to grant the dollar credit we were asking for.

We deliberately waited a few days before asking the President to receive Prince Bertil. When we did so, the answer from the White House came immediately.

'Audience' is a misleading word to use about Roosevelt. Once you had passed all the guards and secretaries and entered the President's study, all formality disappeared. Anyhow, this was the case when the visitor was Prince Bertil.

'Hello, my dear Bert,' was the President's greeting.

Roosevelt has the gift of giving his visitor the definite impression that nothing in the world could be more interesting to him. He listens intently. When he is amused he throws his head back and laughs boisterously.

The President questioned the Prince about his mission and listened to an account of our tentative efforts to buy armaments, including aeroplanes.

'Speak to the Assistant Secretary of the Army,' he advised us and turning to his inseparable companion, General Watson, he added, 'Ring Bill (or Jack or Fred) and tell him to help the Prince.'

The answer came: 'Engines for aeroplanes? Well, I believe that the British and the French have fully booked the output of the factories in Buffalo. But I can always speak to the director.'

To my astonishment, the President himself put in the telephone call to Buffalo. While he waited, he talked about the Air Forces in Europe. He has little confidence in the French Air Force, thinks the German Air Force incomparably the most powerful in the world, but believes that the British now have under construction aeroplanes perhaps better than the German.

Then followed a long monologue on the world situation. He takes a gloomy view of Europe. He believes that the present military stagnation will soon be broken. He indicated with words and gestures that he doubted the ability of France to stand fast against Hitler.

He sank deeper down in his armchair. 'The coming spring and summer,' he said in his deep voice, rubbing his clean-cut chin. 'The coming spring and summer . . .' He didn't finish the sentence.

Suddenly he shook himself. His expression changed from stern seriousness to the more usual happy smile.

'Well, Prince, is there anything else I can do for you?'

The Prince hesitated a moment. Then he said: 'Yes, we are interested in a cruiser.'

'A cruiser,' exclaimed the President delightedly. He glanced at the pictures of ships decorating his library.

'What sort of a cruiser?' he asked with intense interest.

The Prince explained. We knew it was more than uncertain whether the United States could part with a cruiser, but if it was at all possible Sweden would be very much interested in acquiring a heavy cruiser. The Prince then gave a quite expert description of the naval situation in the Baltic.

[131]

The President interrupted him in his eagerness.

'Yes, I know,' he said. 'The Germans have two pocket battle-ships with 28-cm guns and also the heavy cruisers *Hipper, Seydlitz* and *Prince Eugen*. They are armed with 20-cm guns. Now let's see. What would you need?' His eyes sparkled with interest. 'Yes, we must obviously consider the distances in the Baltic.'

He shouted to Watson, 'Pa, take down *Jane's Fighting Ships* from the shelf, and the map of the Baltic in the atlas on the left there.'

While the General got the books, the President turned towards us.

'I've given away cruisers once before,' he said pensively. 'When I was Assistant Secretary of the Navy in 1913 I got President Wilson to agree to give two cruisers to Greece. I'm inclined to believe that otherwise war would have broken out between Greece and Turkey.

'Well, here we have our battleships,' he said with *Jane's Fighting Ships* in his hands. 'I know almost all of them personally, but it is safer to have the pictures to look at. The Missouri class is, of course, far too heavy for the Baltic. The Pennsylvania class is too old.'

He turned the pages of the heavy book. It was obvious that he took great pleasure in looking at the pictures of ships. He became absorbed in questions of naval construction. He discussed gun turrets, speeds, fuel consumption . . . I had the feeling he could go on for hours.

Suddenly he exclaimed: 'This is the one! This is precisely what would suit you!' With a triumphant smile he put a picture before us. *Pensacola*, we read. We contemplated the picture with due respect. The President became engrossed in details. *Pensacola* was ten years old, a cruiser of 9000 tons, armed with ten 20-cm guns. She had good speed—32 knots.

'I've heard that both *Pensacola* and her sister ship *Salt Lake City* are apt to roll at low speed,' the President explained. 'You will have to let her make high speed even if it is a bit narrow in the Baltic.'

'All this sounds absolutely wonderful,' Prince Bertil remarked with a happy smile. 'But how do we acquire her?'

'Acquire her?' the President said pensively. 'That's quite another story. Personally I would like Sweden to have her. She might help to keep the peace in the Baltic. But I'm only the President of this country.' He laughed. 'There is very little I can do. The Congress must give its permission before I can give you a cruiser.'

We waited in silence. The President was obviously considering a plan of campaign.

'It isn't going to be easy,' he said at last. 'But it might be amusing to have a try. Let me see . . . Have you spoken to Cordell Hull?' We said we hadn't spoken to anybody.

'Just as well, perhaps.' The President smiled. 'But the first step has to be a talk with Cordell,' he explained. 'I don't know what he will say. I really never know with him. But it is necessary to get his support. It is up to you to talk to him.'

Some days later the Prince and I were received by the Secretary of State.

The old State Department has a rather depressing exterior. It reminds me of some of the old hotels in Montreux or Vevey. But the interior is friendly; the old black office-keepers and the swinging doors give it an atmosphere of the Southern states—somewhat untidy, even ramshackle, but friendly.

Cordell Hull was seated at an immense desk more encumbered with papers, files and books than any surface I have seen. There was only a little square just in front of him which was free of papers. There Mr Hull rested his long thin hands, while leaning his fine Senator's head backwards and looking absently into the air.

After a moment of silence, he stood up to greet the Prince. Smiling gently, he asked some questions about Sweden and Finland, but it seemed to me that he hardly listened to the answers. Instead he began slowly to speak as if to himself. He spoke about peace. This was his main interest, he said. A democratic peace without conquests and in the spirit of brotherhood. There must be general disarmament, he said, and with raised voice added, 'Disarmament not only in military matters but also in customs and tariffs.' When he spoke of tariff reductions, his eyes sparkled and he made an impatient gesture towards the heaps of paper on his desk, as if he wanted to sweep them away together with tariffs and all other irrational obstacles to human happiness.

It was difficult for the Prince to find an opening. Then came a moment when Hull stopped his monologue and brooded in silence on the grim mistakes made at the World Economic Conference of 1933.

'We would very much like to discuss the desire of the Swedish Government to acquire a cruiser,' the Prince said firmly.

'I beg your pardon?' Mr Hull shook himself. 'A cruiser?' He sounded surprised and reproachful.

The Prince explained. He spoke of our military needs in general and of our Baltic Navy. Hull showed no interest. The Prince mentioned that the President had shown a positive interest. Hull still looked at the ceiling.

'It is all for the sake of peace,' the Prince said. 'I sincerely believe that the addition of a heavy cruiser to the Swedish Navy would substantially help the peace in the Baltic.'

Hull regarded him intently. He had become interested. Then he leaned back in his chair and stressing each word he said, 'Yes, Prince, if it's a question of peace I am with you. If the cruiser can secure peace in the Baltic I am ready to give my assent.'

He suddenly stood up and bowed his head. The audience had come to an end.

As we left he raised both hands in the air, saying, 'God bless you, folks.'

When the President was told that the Secretary of State agreed to Sweden having an American cruiser, he advised us to speak to Senator Pittman of Nevada, chairman of the Foreign Affairs Committee of the Senate. The Swedish Minister invited the Senator to dinner.

Senator Pittman has long been a leading member of the powerful Foreign Affairs Committee, but surprisingly few foreigners have met him. Pittman wasn't born in the mountains of Nevada but in Missouri, and educated in the Deep South. He is, by profession, a lawyer. But, perhaps because he did not have sufficient success in that profession, he became a gold-digger in Alaska. After some years in the goldfields, he returned to the law, this time in Nevada. This state, with the smallest population in the Union, has two leading cities, Reno and Las Vegas, and they are in competition. Reno has the lead in divorces and Las Vegas in gambling.

Pittman became one of the two senators for the state of Nevada in 1913 and eventually he became the senator with the longest service. Nobody has more respect for seniority than American senators.

All this doesn't imply that Pittman lays claim to special knowledge of foreign countries and conditions. He has never been abroad and he only reluctantly visits New York.

He is a friendly man. After dinner he sat down comfortably in a corner with Prince Bertil and in his rich Southern drawl told amusing stories while he refilled his glass of whisky with a trained hand. He is the only man I have seen emptying in one draught a large glass full of neat whisky. He is sixty-eight years old.

When the Prince spoke of the cruiser, Pittman looked grave. He asked for details. With a broad gesture he indicated that he realized that the Baltic was connected with the Atlantic and that therefore a cruiser—even a heavy one—would be able to enter this distant sea. He had lived many years in Alaska, he said, so he had much experience of wild and unhospitable countries. But he would like to know more about Sweden's situation, its political system and its neighbours.

He was a Democrat, he emphasized. He had no sympathy with the Nazis. He seemed to distrust the Soviets even more. On the whole he pitied us Swedes for having been placed in such a nasty corner.

The Prince explained the naval situation at great length.

The Senator was interested. It was obvious that he felt sympathy towards this young Prince who had come such a long way to speak to Senator Pittman from Nevada.

The Prince mentioned that the President had shown a positive attitude. This made no impression on the Senator.

The Prince said that Cordell Hull had promised to help. The Senator sat up and asked if he had heard correctly. When the Prince repeated that Hull had promised his help, Pittman suddenly looked very resolute and declared that he also was ready to give his support.

The Senator then relaxed into his anecdotal mood and we sat in a circle around him listening to his stories, of which he had an unlimited supply and at which no one laughed louder than he did—sometimes, I'm afraid, before we had grasped the point.

The President was more than satisfied when the Prince reported to him.

'That's more than I could ever have got from Pittman,' he said. 'But the next step will be even more difficult. Now you will have to speak to the Republican leader in the Committee for Foreign Affairs,

Senator Vandenberg. If you can persuade him to support your proposal, you can take over my job as President.'

Prince Bertil set out to find the Senator from Michigan. As I had a meeting in New York in connection with the dollar loan I was not present when they met. Senator Vandenberg is generally considered to be the leader of American isolationism, taking his stand with both feet strictly within the narrow circle of the American neutrality legislation.

After he had listened attentively to Prince Bertil and put some questions, he thought deeply for a while and then declared that he 'wouldn't oppose the proposal so long as nobody else opposed it'.

This was surely one of the triumphs of Swedish diplomacy.

Even the most sceptical of us Swedes (meaning myself) began to feel we really had achieved our objective. The President of the United States had given his assent and devoted much time to help us along. The Secretary of State had promised his support. Of the two vital Senators, one had given his blessing and the other declared that he wouldn't oppose the proposal.

When we reported the news about Vandenburg to the President he seemed almost incredulous.

'Did Vandenberg really say this,' Roosevelt mumbled to himself. 'Well, who knows? Everything is possible. Perhaps you will get your cruiser at last.'

He threw his head back and laughed heartily. Then, after a moment, he said, 'But now the most difficult part remains. It is the very last obstacle. You must speak to Hiram Johnson, the Senator from California. I can't help you in any way.'

It took us a few days to get in touch with Senator Johnson. This seventy-five-year-old Senator seemed to lead a life very much by himself in a distant bungalow. Our enthusiasm after Prince Bertil's meeting with Vandenberg was ebbing slightly. I had all sorts of trouble over details in the agreement on the dollar loan. The news from Scandinavia was more and more disquieting.

Late one afternoon when I returned to the Hotel Mayflower, I found Prince Bertil in a sorrowful mood. 'The bubble has burst at last,' he said. 'It was quite impossible to get anywhere with that Senator from California. As soon as I mentioned the word "cruiser" he sat up in his chair and snapped, "Well, Prince, I'm bound to say it at once: I am *dead* against it." Then I had to talk about something else.'

President Roosevelt smiled when the Prince gave him the news.

'Yes, yes,' he sighed. 'There you can see for yourselves how it is to be President of the United States.' He sat silent for a while, then he said in a deeply serious voice, 'You see it takes a long, long time to bring the past up to the present.'

The Prince and I agreed that the most painful part was going to be informing dear Admiral Wijkmark. Cautiously, we opened the door to his office. There he sat writing a list of the naval personnel needed for *Pensacola*.

The Prince told him as tactfully as possible that Senator Hiram Johnson didn't sympathize with our wish to acquire *Pensacola* for the Swedish Navy. The President, the Secretary of State, the leaders of the two parties simply had to bow to the decision of the Senator from California.

The Admiral was silent. Trying to be consoling, I said, 'But it has always been very unlikely that we would get the cruiser. The irritating thing is that after the conversation with Vandenberg, we began to have some hopes.'

'Not me,' the Admiral replied with a little smile. 'I never really believed it.'

'What?' I retorted almost indignantly. 'It's you who's been for ever talking about the cruiser. Not a day has passed without your discussing the qualities and the defects of *Pensacola*. If you never believed in the project, why have you spent days and nights over your plans for the cruiser?'

'No, I never believed we would get *Pensacola*,' the Admiral repeated. And smiling his quiet smile he went on: 'You will understand me if I say that it was such happiness for an old sailor like me to plan and prepare for a real cruiser.' Then he added with a sigh, 'I will miss *Pensacola*.'

X

The Ninth of April

One morning in New York I sat at the breakfast table contemplating a cartoon in the *New York Times*. It showed a vastly inflated Hitler locked in a room with windows too small for him to get out. The caption read 'Blown up and nowhere to go'.

I thought this the most misleading cartoon comment ever made. Was not the truth of the matter really that we were all waiting anxiously to see where Hitler would decide to throw in his armies? His military supremacy seemed to me so overwhelming that I believed him capable of attacking in almost any direction he chose.

But the cartoon was probably significant of the beliefs held by many people in Western countries. Our delegates in London had told me that many of the British leaders believed that Germany was having serious difficulties in meeting her needs of metals, iron ore and oil. They thought Hitler was hesitating in face of the risks of an attack on the Maginot Line and that the war might well end in the summer of 1940. I had encountered similar opinions in many quarters in America. One of the very few who took an opposite view was President Roosevelt. When Prince Bertil and I called on him a few days after the conclusion of the peace treaty between Finland and the Soviet Union, the President, as usual, expressed his opinion very openly. He smiled at all the criticism—not to say the insults—directed against Sweden as an instigator of the peace. 'It was wise to make peace,' he said. 'The most important thing, of course, was to prevent the Western Powers from coming into the war against the Russians.'

This last remark seemed to me essential. How was it possible that a British government could seriously contemplate sending troops to Finland to fight the Soviet Union? Was it not that the British, under the inspiration of Winston Churchill, simply wanted to spread the war? The troops would have been intended not only to stop the exports of iron ore but to create a new battle-front in Scandinavia as a diversion from the Western Front.

[138]

On my return to Stockholm towards the end of March I called on the Foreign Minister, Günther, and congratulated him on the part he had played in bringing the Finns and the Russians to the negotiating table. With his usual modesty, he said, 'One must have a bit of luck to succeed'. He thought it was now reasonable to hope that the threat of war over Scandinavia would diminish, the pretext for a Western intervention having disappeared.

But when I met Jacob Wallenberg to discuss our forthcoming negotiations with the Germans he gave me a very different appreciation of the situation. He reminded me of what he had told me in December about German plans for military action against Scandinavia. Since the beginning of March he had seen many signs of preparations for such an action.

Only a few days before my return to Stockholm a German military delegation had been there to discuss future German sales of arms to Sweden. After a dinner party the German officers had stayed late over coffee and brandy and one of them had given Wallenberg clear hints of a German attack on Denmark and Norway in the very near future. Wallenberg had, of course, reported this conversation to the Swedish Foreign Office.

A few days later I received a message from Berlin that the Germans wanted to postpone our negotiations. I took this as another sign.

In the first days of April there was a flood of telegrams and letters from the Swedish Legation in Berlin warning us of a German attack on Denmark and Norway. In the Foreign Office, however, there were many who didn't believe the warnings. They pointed to various earlier warnings of forthcoming attacks on Belgium, Holland and France, which had proved groundless.

On April 6, the two young princes, Bertil and Carl Johan, came to my office. They wanted to hear my opinion. I said I found the news from Berlin very menacing. 'That is also the opinion of the old man,'* Bertil said. 'When the Government refused to call for mobilization he was so incensed that he broke one of the finest pieces of his Chinese collection.' As usual the Prince was very refreshing. He declared that he would be delighted to lead his flotilla of motor torpedo-boats against the German ships in the Sound. 'I'll be damned if we wouldn't sink a lot of those bloody Germans,' he exclaimed.

* Their father, the Crown Prince, Gustaf Adolf (born 1882). He became King of Sweden in 1950.

Then, on April 9, it was as if a thunderbolt had struck us. We stood in a group round the loudspeaker in the Foreign Ministry. As more and more telegrams were read in the course of the morning the picture of the wave of German attacks became clearer and even more horrifying. When I heard of the attempts of the few guards outside the Royal Palace in Copenhagen to put up a fight against the German invaders, I couldn't restrain my tears.

Soon we had to return to our work and it was only late in the evening that I could sit down and think about the situation. According to my habit I wrote down what I thought:

Obviously one's thoughts go first to our Scandinavian neighbours and their sufferings. At the same time one has to admit that Munch and other protagonists of disarmament have a heavy responsibility. If the Danes had been able to defend their airfields for even a day the situation would have been less catastrophic. Isolated disarmament is a treason against one's neighbours.

If the Germans haven't attacked Sweden it must mean that their aim is to prevent a Western intervention in the north of Scandinavia. But how can the Germans possibly conquer and keep Narvik in face of the whole British Navy? Yet if they fail, which seems likely, that would mean the Allies would intervene in northern Norway and the Germans would then be obliged to fight their way through Sweden to tackle the Allies in Norway. Our situation seems to me extremely menacing.

This was my assessment on the evening of April 9. The following days were quickly to show how wrong I had been. The Germans succeeded in carrying through their unbelievably daring attack on Narvik.

In the afternoon of April 14 I was called urgently to the Foreign Minister. In his waiting-room I found Admiral Tamm, Knut Dahlberg, Rolf von Heidenstam, Sven Tunberg and Birger Dahlerus. When I greeted them Dahlberg whispered to me: 'So you will come with us on this "Hacha-journey".' (A little more than a year earlier Hacha, the President of Czechoslovakia, had been summoned to Hitler and forced to sign a declaration abolishing the independence of his country.)

When we saw the Foreign Minister he read a telegram from the

Legation in Berlin. Field-Marshal Göring had expressed the wish to meet very soon special representatives of the Swedish Government. The Foreign Minister was very laconic. He simply said that we had to leave early the following day.

We five delegates met in the evening. Dahlerus, who had recently seen Göring, considered it very important that we should put to him arguments he could use to calm down Hitler. The Führer was very suspicious of Sweden. He thought we had a secret understanding with the British. I pointed out that the Swedish Government had already declared several times its firm intention to defend the Swedish frontiers against any aggressor. We telephoned to Günther, who instructed us to make the same declaration to Göring.

We left early the following morning. In the aeroplane I sat thinking about Göring. During the first years of the Nazis I had, as I have recorded earlier, seen him fairly often with Hitler and Goebbels in the Hotel Kaiserhof. There too I had watched his fantastic wedding party; watched him, in his resplendent white uniform, and his Junoesque bride, acknowledge from a balcony the thunderous cheers of tens of thousands of Berliners crowding the Wilhemsplatz. Later I watched the wedding reception in the great hall of the hotel. Beside the bride and bridegroom sat Hitler, in Nazi uniform, the nearly ninety-year-old Field-Marshal von Mackensen in the black uniform of his 'death's-head' Hussar regiment, Doctor Schacht and most of the rest of the Nazi hierarchy. When the orchestra began to play a *Rheinlander* the massive bridal couple lumbered across the dance floor.

Yet this man whom I had found so comical in his musical comedy costume was now the second man in the most powerful and most menacing state in Europe. Recently Hitler had appointed him *Schwedenreferent*, responsible for the relations with Sweden.

I asked Dahlerus, who was sitting beside me, how he had come to know Göring. It was a curious story. Some years ago Dahlerus had married a German lady of a well-known and rich patrician family in Hamburg. Among the Nazi party in Hamburg there was a group of SA men who used their power for all sorts of blackmail and the only thing to do when threatened was to pay up or find 'protection'—which meant somebody high up in the Nazi Party. Dahlerus thought of Göring, whose first wife was Swedish and, equipped with letters of introduction from relatives of the deceased Frau Göring, he succeeded in obtaining an appointment with the Field-Marshal. When he had told his story Göring wanted to throw him out. Dahlerus had 'insulted the Nazi Party by his accusations against the SA in Hamburg'. With his natural gift for dramatizing a situation, Dahlerus protested that he was ready to go to prison if it could be proved that his accusations were unfounded. Göring had appreciated this 'manful frankness', an investigation was made and the SA group in Hamburg were arrested. So Dahlerus became a friend of Göring.

In the afternoon of April 15 we were received by Göring in his gigantic Air Ministry in Berlin. He was attended by two of his highest officials. Admiral Tamm sat opposite Göring and I on Tamm's right. Göring seemed even broader and heavier than before. His white uniform was too tight round the waist. I was fascinated by an enormous ruby on the middle finger of his left hand. The jewel flashed when he made sweeping gestures as he expounded his version of the war situation.

The Western Powers were trying to create a crisis in the supply of raw materials to Germany. They aimed at provoking internal unrest in Germany and finally at breaking through on one front or another. Their first goals were to stop the deliveries of oil from Romania and iron ore from Sweden. They would then try to destroy the German industrial centre in the Ruhr.

Through their Secret Service, the Germans had learned that at the Anglo-French ministerial meeting in London it had been decided to occupy Trondheim and Bergen on the Atlantic coast of Norway. The plans had been prepared in detail. The Germans had succeeded in forestalling them by only eight hours.

Germany had no interest in dragging Scandinavia into the war. On the contrary, Germany preferred to leave Scandinavia in peace. It was the British who had tried to spread the war in the north as in the south of Europe. As the Norwegian military organization was miserably inadequate, the Germans had decided that Norway was unable to defend her neutrality.

Turning to Sweden, Göring explained that Germany had no interest in seeing our country turned into a battlefield. Denmark and Norway were now in 'strong German hands' (*in fester deutscher Hand*). They would henceforth form a wall against the Western Allies. There was, however, a possibility that the German troops around Narvik would find themselves in a difficult situation because of the harsh winter and the mountainous country. The British might perhaps be able to push the German divisions back so that they could advance to the Swedish frontier and from there to the iron-ore mines.

Was Sweden ready to prevent such an aggression? Or was it Sweden's secret intention to defend the frontier only in theory? In some German quarters it was always said that Sweden was in connivance with England and would acquiesce in an occupation of the iron-ore fields.

Over and over again Göring came back to this question. It was of decisive importance that Germany receive assurances of Sweden's willingness and readiness effectively to oppose an attempt to cross the Swedish frontier. If such an assurance were given, he, Göring, would 'take an oath on his honour as soldier and Field-Marshal' that Sweden would not be made the object of any German military measures.

By now Göring had been speaking for more than an hour. I had glanced at Admiral Tamm, a signal that he should deliver our assurance. But Tamm was probably right in keeping silent. Göring obviously felt a need to pour out his words and to listen to his own voice.

When at last Tamm intervened he declared in a loud voice that Sweden's policy was to defend Sweden's neutrality with the utmost vigour against any aggressor. This was the absolute will of the Swedish people and this declaration was a declaration of the Swedish Government.

Immediately Göring stood up and pressed the Admiral's hand. In his most dramatic manner he said that the Swedish declaration was of decisive importance. He would immediately inform Hitler.

Göring then began to warn us of British manoeuvres. There had been 'countless British secret agents in Norway' who would now doubtless start working in Sweden. I said that we did not have the impression that the British really intended to make an attack on the iron-ore mines. Anyhow, Sweden had quite sufficient military forces to prevent such an attack.

The following day we left Berlin to visit Göring's country residence, Karinhalle (named after his Swedish first wife, Karin). It had originally been a relatively simple house for Göring's shooting parties in the vast surrounding forests. Now it was a sumptuous mansion.

We were received by Göring's first aide, General Bodenschatz, who explained that Göring was still in conference with Hitler, so he would show us round the house.

Göring's study was an immense room, obviously inspired by Mussolini's famous office in the Palazzo Venezia. There was a large portrait of Bismarck; Hitler was represented only by a small photograph. In the broad corridor outside the study we admired a set of magnificent tapestries. I remarked to Bodenschatz that they reminded me of tapestries I had seen in a museum in Vienna some years ago. At this moment Göring entered briskly—obviously in a very good mood. He had heard my remark and replied immediately, 'But they are the same. The city of Vienna has given them to me as a present'. *

Göring now took over our conducted tour. With obvious delight he showed us his collection of shooting outfits. One was in the old Norse style, which would make the wearer look like the god Odin. Another was clearly inspired by Lohengrin.

In another great room Göring had built a system of miniature railways and he himself directed the toy trains through tunnels and over mountains, switching on and off innumerable red and green lights. He laughed with pleasure as he showed us all sorts of small gadgets which he claimed to have invented himself.

Finally we came to a gallery where we sat down at a luncheon table. Göring opened a cupboard, took out a bottle of Swedish schnapps and filled our glasses and his own. Only Bodenschatz was left out.

Soon Göring began to talk about the situation in Norway. Like all the leading Nazis, he couldn't refrain from seemingly endless monologues. It was only when he put direct questions that he stopped speaking for a few moments. When he had finished his monologue on Norway, he started to criticize the Swedish press. Hitler read Swedish newspapers every day, he said. The Führer found that the Swedish press was the most anti-German in the whole world. If

---

* Later a German friend told me that Göring had a habit of letting local authorities and boards of industrial companies and banks know that he would appreciate this or that work of art as a token of respect. This almost always had the desired effect. It seems that Hitler was irritated by Göring's methods as an art collector.

measures were not taken to moderate the Swedish newspapers' attacks on Germany it could lead to an explosion.

Back in Berlin, Admiral Tamm was due to be received by Hitler. Tamm, with his tall, heavy figure, his swinging sailor's stride and his hearty laughter, usually gave the impression of being perfectly sure of himself. But this time was different. 'I tell you frankly,' he said to me, 'I am damned nervous.'

When he returned from the interview he sank down in an armchair with a sigh. 'You know,' he said, 'I am dead-beat.' Hitler had been tough from the start. He had shouted that he had to crush every obstacle—and that would apply to Sweden too, if necessary. Göring often spoke in favour of Sweden, but one could not rely too much on him because of his Swedish marriage and Swedish sympathies. Turning to the situation in Norway, Hitler said that all Norway, with the possible exception of the Narvik area and the railway line to Sweden, would soon be occupied.

Here Tamm managed to interrupt for the first time in more than half an hour. He repeated his declaration that Sweden was ready to defend her frontiers against an aggressor. Hitler shouted, 'And does this also apply to England?' Yes, Tamm said, it did. But Hitler doubted it. He asked, 'Who is saying this? Is it the King?' Tamm replied: 'It is the King, the Government and the Swedish people.'

Hitler's mood now changed. In a friendly vein he began a new monologue about Germany and Sweden's contributions to the maintenance of the Germanic race. He would like to believe that the Swedes were still good soldiers. In any case Germany had no interest in having Sweden as an opponent.

Next day we flew back to Stockholm to report to the Government. The following weeks were full of work. I was responsible for two negotiations, one with the Germans and the other with the Russians.

On May 9 I was suddenly summoned by the Foreign Minister, who told me that I had to leave the following morning with Admiral Tamm and Dahlerus for another meeting with Göring.

Our aeroplane was held up in Malmoe. The great German attack on the West had started that morning. We spent the day walking in Malmoe, but it was impossible to think of anything except the storm of steel and blood now sweeping across the heartlands of Western civilization.

In the evening Dahlerus described to me a conversation he had had with Göring a few days earlier, and which explained why we were making our present journey. Göring had been very angry. Over and over again he repeated that Sweden had to understand that we had now entered a period when the small states had to accept the leadership of the Great Powers. Sweden's defences were worthless. Sweden didn't have the slightest chance of preventing a German occupation.

After this pleasant introduction Göring had explained that the German troops round Narvik were in difficulty. But Hitler refused to give up. On the contrary, he had given orders that everything should be done to prevent a reverse. Göring then made the following proposal: the Swedish Government should permit the passage through Sweden of artillery and ammunition in railway wagons with Red Cross markings, or, alternatively, the Swedish Government should sell three artillery batteries to Germany, to be delivered at the frontier near Narvik, against a sale of three German batteries to be delivered in Sweden. If the Swedish Government didn't accept one of these two proposals it would be obvious to the Führer that Sweden was an enemy of Germany. He did not need to describe the far-reaching consequences for Sweden.

Dahlerus answered that he did not believe the Swedish Government would accept either of the two alternatives.

It was against this background that Dahlerus had proposed that a Swedish delegation should be sent to discuss the matter with Göring.

We arrived in Berlin on May 11. Richert, our Minister there, was as calm as ever, but he confirmed that there were widespread rumours of concentrations of troops against Sweden.

We were driven at shattering speed to Göring's headquarters, some hundred kilometres to the west of Berlin. The headquarters consisted of two long railway trains sited near an airfield. When we arrived we saw Göring standing between the two trains, surrounded by a group of Air Force generals among whom I recognized General Milch.

Göring was beaming and we gathered he had been listening to the

[146]

latest reports on the gigantic raids carried out by the German Air Force in Belgium and Holland.

In the usual Nazi manner he launched into a long monologue. Already—after only twenty-four hours—it was clear that Holland was collapsing. Belgium would soon follow. At the same time a hundred German divisions would cross Luxembourg into France and crush the French armies. This would be accomplished in six or eight weeks. The German Air Force would be able to dominate the Channel from their bases on the French coast. England would then make peace. Germany had no intention of destroying England or the British Empire. In any case, it was the firm intention of Germany to finish the war before the end of the year.

Göring now turned to the question of Narvik. The attack on Narvik was a personal decision of Hitler's. The military staffs had been very much against it. Hitler would never forgive Sweden if the German heroes of Narvik were to perish because of Sweden's stubborn refusal to permit the transit of arms and ammunition. Sweden had not refused such transit to Finland during the winter war. The minimum requirement, Göring said, was that Sweden should not harm Germany's vital interests through a one-sided and anti-German application of neutrality.

Admiral Tamm now delivered a very laconic declaration that the Swedish Government was not willing to permit the transit of arms.

Göring was clearly surprised by this categorical statement. He sank deeper in his armchair. Then he began to speak with increasing vehemence. I tried to explain to him that Sweden had never declared herself neutral in the war between Russia and Finland. Our attitude to the war in Norway was very different.

Göring asked (with a sniff at me) if this meant that Sweden blockaded her frontiers with Norway. I answered that we made a distinction between civilian goods and war materials. But, Göring exclaimed, such a distinction was meaningless under modern conditions. It was really high time that Sweden understood the seriousness of the situation and applied her neutrality in a sensible way.

'I know you well, you Swedes! You sit there in your corner waiting to see if perhaps England is going to win in the end. But I assure you, you're wrong. We are not going to let the war drag on. That was the mistake we made last time. We will finish this war before the end of the year.'

[147]

I repeated that the Swedish Government did not consider that the transit of war material to an army invading Norway was consistent with our neutrality. The Field-Marshal became purple in the face and shouted at me, 'You, Herr Hagglof, are an incorrigible lawyer and diplomat. You understand nothing of the great problems of the destiny of nations'. *

This outburst was accompanied by a bang on the table with his clenched fist.

After a few moments of silence Göring rang for his aide, the young Major von Brauchitz, and, leaning on his arm, left the room.

Admiral Tamm whispered to me, 'Listen. This is all going to hell. But what the devil can we do?'

After a while Göring returned. He looked much calmer. (He had probably had a fresh injection of morphia.) I started to explain how the Swedish and Norwegian peoples were closely related; innumerable Swedes had close bonds with Norway through family and friendship. It would be against every rule of honour and decency to permit the transit of arms in Norway's present tragic situation.

Tamm backed me up by saying that for us to permit the transit of arms would be felt as a disgrace by the Swedish people.

Göring declared that he had not intended to threaten Sweden. But nothing could be easier than to force Sweden to comply. The German Air Force could destroy a number of centres in Sweden without any difficulty. The Swedish Government would then quickly accept his terms.

So the talk continued for a while. Then suddenly the Field-Marshal stood up, bringing the discussion to an abrupt end.

On our return to Stockholm Admiral Tamm and I made our report to the Government. When I finished, Tamm asked if he might make what he called a 'personal declaration'. First he spoke of the photographs which Göring had shown us of German air attacks on British cruisers off the Norwegian coast. They showed that the German Air Force was capable of eliminating the British Navy even in waters traditionally considered to be Britain's. Now, the Admiral continued, it seemed that the German Air Force was also well on its way to eliminating the armies of the Western Allies. He declared that

* 'Sie, Herr Hägglöf, sind ein einge fleischter Jurist und Diplomat, Sie verstehen nichts von den grossen Schicksalsfragen der Völker.'

as a professional 'military' man he must come to the conclusion that Germany was going to win the war. He considered it to be his duty to give the Government his opinion with complete frankness.

There was a dead silence after this declaration. Then the Prime Minister indicated with a gesture that the meeting was at an end.

As we walked out Tamm explained that he hadn't forewarned me of his intention to make this declaration as he knew that I was not of the same opinion. I replied that I thought it much too early to make prognostications about the final outcome. The war between the Great Powers had just started. Tamm retorted that it was already quite clear that the British Navy was in a precarious position because of the German Air Force's strength, and that the Allied armies were already in disorder.

We were interrupted by a messenger calling me to see the Prime Minister. When I entered his room he asked, 'What have you to say about Tamm's declaration?' I repeated what I had just told Tamm. It was much too early to draw any conclusions about the final outcome of the war. Obviously it had to be admitted that so far the Germans had demonstrated a clear superiority. But Göring had said that Germany would not make the same mistake as in 1914–18 by letting the war drag on year after year. This time they were decided to make it a short war. Göring had said he was convinced of a German victory before the end of the year. This indicated that he feared the war could turn out badly for Germany if it dragged on.

The P.M. listened. He sighed deeply. 'The outlook is damned black,' he said. 'But under no circumstances can we go back on our refusal to allow the transit to Narvik.'

Some days later the German Foreign Minister, von Ribbentrop, made pressing demands for the transit to Narvik. He spoke in a very threatening way to the Swedish Minister in Berlin. When the Government repeated its refusal, the situation seemed exceedingly serious.

At the end of May and the beginning of June I was in Berlin for negotiations with the German permanent delegation. Early each morning I sat in my room in the Kaiserhof listening to the radio. It became clearer every day that the Germans were annihilating the French armies. But there was no atmosphere of victory in Berlin. My opposite number Herr Walter—one of Germany's most able and experienced civil servants—sometimes discussed with me the events in France. His conclusion was simple: 'Now we can hope for peace in September.' This seemed to be the general opinion in the Ministries and among bankers and industrialists.

Still heavy clouds remained massed over Sweden. When I spoke to Ambassador Ritter, who was the Foreign Ministry's representative at Hitler's headquarters, he repeated the warning that the Führer would never allow the 'heroes of Narvik' to perish because of Sweden's obstinacy over the transit of arms. He was ready to use any means in his power to save the German troops at Narvik.

I was visited at the Kaiserhof by various Germans I had reason to regard as sincere friends of Sweden. They all gave me the same warnings. 'Hitler can attack Sweden at any moment. Why not make a concession before it is too late? Remember that France will soon be totally defeated. The war will be won by the autumn. It is much more in the long-term interest of Scandinavia to make this concession and so avoid the devastation of Sweden than to persist in your stubborn refusal.'

Over and over again I had to explain the reasons for our refusal. I was personally convinced that we had to maintain our stand. But I confess that there were days and nights when I expected the telephone to ring with a message that the German attack on Sweden had begun.

When Jacob Wallenberg and I returned to Stockholm in early June we were greeted with the news that the Norwegian Government and Allied troops were evacuating Norway and were being shipped to England.

The threat hanging over Sweden since our meeting with Göring on May 11 disappeared at once. I confess that I sighed a sigh of relief. The four weeks of waiting had been a time of agony.

XI
Germany's Victory Summer

The German victories came in quick succession. Göring's forecast at our meeting of May 11 was coming true. After a campaign of four weeks the French armies were breaking up. On June 17 Marshal Pétain asked for an armistice.

I was in Berlin negotiating with the German Foreign Ministry. The streets were almost empty. In the hall of the Kaiserhof Hotel people sat all day listening to the loud-speakers repeating every half-hour the reports from France. It was victory all the way. Yet there was no over-excited flush of triumph among the people I met; the most my German opposite numbers sometimes allowed themselves to say was that we could now hope for peace in the autumn. This, was, of course, exactly what Göring had said: the Führer would not repeat the folly of 1914–1918 by letting the war drag on. It must be brought to an end this year.

During the summer it became clear that the Germans were preparing for the coming 'peace'. In the armament industries they were already worrying about a post-war slump. They were looking for long-term orders from Sweden. I learned later that the Government wanted to buy vast quantities of Swedish granite blocks to be used for grandiose buildings to celebrate their victory.

In discussions about relations between Sweden and Germany after the victory it was pointed out to us that Sweden would be in a position of great dependence on German industries. Britain would have entirely lost her old economic influence in Sweden. Therefore, they said, was it not clear that Sweden should now consider herself free of any obligations towards Britain under current treaties? I answered that these treaties, some of which were three hundred years old, were certainly still fully valid.

It was still possible to give such firm answers. But how long would it be possible? That was the question tormenting one's mind.

In the seven years since 1933 the whole European scene had completely changed. Poland had been crushed. Denmark and Norway

were 'in firm German hands'. Belgium, Holland and even France
had been crushed after only a few weeks of struggle.

Only Britain was still on her feet. But for how long? The German
Air Force had shown its terrific power both on land and sea. The
British Army had been saved from Dunkirk almost miraculously,
but had they not lost their guns and a great deal of their other
armaments?

I sat one evening discussing the dark prospect with my old
friend Eric von Rosen. We were joined at dinner by Frans G. Bengt-
son, a well-known writer and staunch Anglophile. Frans listened for
a while to the gloomy reflections of Eric and myself. Then he started
to talk in his inimitable way. He told us the story of an English knight
in the Middle Ages who went to Spain seeking conquests. The knight
and his squires were soon surrounded by an overwhelming number
of Spanish knights, who shouted to the English that they had no
earthly chance and must surrender. But the English were so stupid
that they didn't understand that they were defeated. They battled
on until the Spaniards became tired and left for more easily won
victories.

It was certainly a relief to listen to Frans, but I couldn't help
asking myself what Sweden's future would be even if Britain succeeded in preventing a German invasion. The whole European continent up to the Russian frontier was dominated by Germany. On
July 18 the *New York Times* wrote that there were now 'only three
islands of liberty' on the European continent—Sweden, Switzerland
and Finland. It would be a miracle, the paper said, if these three
states were able to keep their heads above water unless Britain soon
defeated the totalitarian powers.

But how could Britain, beleaguered as she was, defeat a Germany
mustering 150 divisions against some tens of British divisions? I
had long been convinced that the Western Powers would never be
able to beat Germany without American participation. I had set my
hopes on Roosevelt. But would he really be re-elected in November?
From my stay in Washington I had learned how much the Americans
hesitated over the idea of a totally unprecedented third term for a
President. And the next point was even more doubtful: would a
re-elected Roosevelt be able to overcome the massive isolationism in
the Congress?

One day at the end of August I talked to the German military attaché in Stockholm, General von Uthmann. We discussed German deliveries of arms to Sweden, and Uthmann explained that the delivery periods would be long; we would not receive any guns until the middle of 1941. With a happy smile he added, 'By then I hope to have been transferred'. I must have looked surprised, for Uthmann started to explain himself. His grandfather had fought as a General in the war against France in 1870. His father had been a General in France during the First World War. He himself had found it very frustrating to remain a military attaché in Sweden while the German armies marched into France for the third time. Therefore he had intimated to his superiors that he was longing for active service, and had been promised his chance. When Uthmann pointed out that the war in France could hardly last much longer, he was told that there were other points of the compass—East, for example. Von Uthmann beamed as he imagined himself leading a Prussian division against Russia.

The attitude of the Germans I dealt with when I was in Berlin in September was simply that if Britain refused to make peace Germany could continue the war in the air indefinitely, as Germany and the German-controlled countries could build many more aeroplanes than Britain. The most important task was to consolidate the German-dominated 'New Order' in Europe: the creation in the next few years of a great European economic unit, which, with Germany as its centre, would rapidly increase production and raise the standard of living. I listened intently, but Jacob Wallenberg and I, who after all were responsible for Sweden's economic relations with Germany, agreed to maintain an entirely passive attitude.

But there were others who felt differently. When I went to Copenhagen to make agreements about Danish–Swedish trade, the new Danish Foreign Minister, Erik Scavenins, explained that Germany would certainly appreciate it very much if a state like Denmark, instead of waiting until Germany had won the war, would announce its willingness to co-operate in the construction of a new Europe. He referred to a declaration made by the Danish Government in July:

The great German victories have struck the world with surprise and admiration. They have ushered in a new period in European history which will lead to a new political and economic order under the leadership of Germany. It will be the task of Denmark to find its place in a necessary and reciprocal co-operation with Greater Germany.

Scavenins, the leader of this very advanced policy of collaboration, was a remarkable man. As Foreign Minister while still in his thirties, he had successfully guided Danish foreign policy throughout the First World War. He was a man of intelligence and much self-assurance. Now, in the present war, he argued that the reason why the Germans had occupied Denmark was in order to have the necessary bases for their 'preventive' attack on Norway.

Once occupied, it was necessary for Denmark to arrange its relations with Germany in such a way that the country would be ruled by its own government and not by Danish Nazis or a German military commander.

I could not follow him in his reasoning, as I objected to the basic principle of his policy—not to defend one's country against aggression. Even if there was no chance of success it seemed to me necessary to put up a fight.

It was, of course, true that in the situation after the fall of France all the smaller states of Europe had to modify their political attitudes to a certain extent. In my economic negotiations with Germany I had to make certain concessions. But when our German opposite numbers began to talk of the coming New Order in Europe Jacob Wallenberg and I refused to budge. We were determined to use every delaying tactic possible.

That, however, did nothing to solve the big question: did we have to count on a German victory?

In my diary of June 1940 I noted that Walter Lippmann had written:

It is our duty to act on the assumption that the Western Allies will lose the war this summer and that we (the U.S.A.)—before the snow has fallen in our country—will stand alone as the last democracy in the world.

It was difficult, if not impossible, to refute this opinion. In Berlin, in Rome, in Vichy—not to speak of the capitals of Central Europe and the Balkans—the governments counted on a victorious German peace by the autumn. The wise and moderate Ernst von Weizsäcker, Secretary of State in the German Foreign Office, said to me that he and his wife planned a long holiday in the winter 'after the conclusion of peace'. Weizsäcker was a sworn enemy of the Nazi régime, but after the resounding German victories in France even he could allow himself to speak with a trace of admiration of Hitler's 'military genius'.

On June 25 Hitler ordered flags to be flown all over Germany for ten days. The churches were to ring their bells for seven days. As I walked the streets of Berlin under streaming Nazi flags and booming church bells I looked with bewildered eyes towards a rapidly darkening future.

Jacob Wallenberg, more experienced than myself, warned me against speculations about the future. He pointed out that we were in a situation so full of uncertain factors that it was better to concentrate on the immediate real problems. In a way it was helpful to be faced with so many practical problems demanding rapid solutions. But I confess that I was often a prey to pessimism. In my diary for August I have a long entry about a conversation with the Foreign Minister:

Günther has returned from his short illness and his holiday. He asked me to report on our German negotiations and agreements and I did so for three-quarters of an hour. Günther asked me when I was going back to Berlin. I said that my German opposite numbers had half-jokingly invited us to a 'victory-feast' in September. That was said in July. Since then the German hopes of a peace with Britain had probably been shattered. We had to wait for German attempts to invade Britain. The attacks from the air are, of course, already in full swing.

Günther made an unusually long speech for him, the result, no doubt, of his thinking while on holiday. He thought it uncertain whether the Germans would succeed in invading Britain. But even if they failed, a country like Sweden will have to reckon with the dominating influence of Germany on Western and Northern Europe. This, he said, would of necessity provoke many and sweeping changes. What could be done to prepare Sweden and Swedish public opinion? Judging by the Swedish press and the debates in the Swedish parliament, one got the impression that the people had no thought of changing their old pattern of life.

He had spoken at great length to the Prime Minister, who had proved very obstinate in spite of the fact that Günther didn't ask for much. He had proposed some Swedish statements showing a willingness to contribute to a new order in Europe with full safeguards for Swedish national interests, some measures to moderate the Swedish press in its denunciations of Germany and the German leaders. To try to change the traditional direction of Sweden's public opinion was a heavy task—like a solitary man trying to turn a heavy barge.

When Günther finished I said that, regretfully, I had to declare myself to be a pessimist. I didn't believe in the possibility of maintaining reasonable relations with a victorious Germany. I was convinced that the Nazi régime, and above all its leader, were determined to change radically not only the map of Europe but also the minds of Europeans.

Günther replied that such an opinion must lead to total despair. He couldn't accept such negativism. We had to try to cultivate the relations we had. He had good and confidential relations with Prince Wied (German Minister in Stockholm). Richert had succeeded in establishing friendly and confidential contacts with men like von Weizsäcker and Grundherr. 'You and Jacob Wallenberg have—as I understand—a great many valuable contacts in Berlin,' he added.

'Yes,' I replied. 'I agree. This is what we can do and what we have to do. But we must be aware of the fact that behind the façade of German civil servants there is the dark volcano of Hitler and his Nazism.'

Günther had told me that he found my assessment of the situation 'negative'. He was right. I couldn't find any glimmer of light in the future as seen from the factual situation in August 1940.

Happily I had a number of concrete tasks to carry on with in the negotiations with both Germany and Britain.

The overall trade agreement we had concluded with Britain in the autumn of 1939 had been fundamentally changed by the German occupation of Denmark and Norway and the German closure of Sweden's access to the North Sea. It seemed that the advantages of

[156]

the agreement—namely British permission for Sweden to import vital supplies from the West—had now disappeared. Nevertheless Marcus Wallenberg, as chairman of the British–Swedish war-trade committee, proposed that Sweden should take a very long-term view and confirm the agreement even in the new situation prevailing after the German breakthrough, and the Government gave its approval, surely a rather daring decision.

However, I carried on long discussions in Berlin with Ambassador Ritter, who was acting as the German blockade Minister. They were not very successful. Ritter turned down my proposals for seaborne traffic between Sweden and America. The Germans wanted to persuade Sweden to start a traffic of blockade-runners. This was, of course, contrary to our basic obligations to Britain.

For days on end I explained that Sweden had to rely on the consent of both the belligerents. Some of the Germans found my attitude stubborn. Ambassador Ritter's first assistant, Schnurre, poured out his feelings in a conversation with the Swedish envoy in Moscow, my old friend Wilhelm Assarsson. Schnurre said that he had been very well received in Stockholm by the Swedish Foreign Minister. But, he said, the leader of the Swedish delegation for Germany, Mr Hagglof, had not shown the same disposition. 'Hagglof didn't seem to understand Hitler's historic mission nor the importance for Sweden of the Führer's taking a benevolent attitude'. When Assarsson pointed out that a neutral country like Sweden had to take into consideration its relations with all the different countries, Schnurre answered, 'You can be certain that people like Hagglof will find one day how totally mistaken they have been'.

XII

Barbarossa *

Can the British stand it? Have they enough troops and arms to beat off a German invasion? These were the questions pounding in our minds in the summer of 1940 as we were faced with daily reports of German air-raids on Britain and repeated warnings of impending invasion.

Above all, we asked ourselves if the British Air Force could defend the island against the powerful and so far always victorious German Air Force?

Then, in early September, I read the news of the British sending several divisions, hundreds of tanks and aeroplanes to Egypt. This must mean, I told myself, that the British leaders considered the defences of the homeland to be so strong that they could spare a great deal for the war in the Middle East.

This news signified to me the end of the summer of German victory and the beginning of an autumn of anxious waiting. On the continent of Europe more than 150 German divisions were standing idle. When and where would Hitler strike next?

As September dragged towards its end, it appeared certain that the German attack on the British Isles had been indefinitely postponed. It seemed hardly likely that they were going to start military operations in the Balkans. They had already sufficient control there. I thought the next move would be a big campaign in North Africa with a view to liquidating the British Empire from Egypt eastwards.

Following the events day by day one slowly got the impression that the German leaders had fallen out of step, that Hitler was hesitating between several alternatives and couldn't make up his mind what to do next. He had had an almost uninterrupted run of success for seven years, culminating in the victory in France. But in September he had been obliged to postpone the long-heralded invasion of Britain. In October he travelled to Brenner to meet Mussolini, to Hendaye to meet Franco, to Montoire to talk to Pétain, and all this without any visible result. At the end of the month Italy launched

* The German code name for the plan for the invasion of Russia.

[158]

an attack on Greece, obviously very much against the wishes of the German leader.

All this pointed to the prolongation of the war. I wondered many times what Göring was thinking. He had been so certain that the war would be over before the end of 1940; was he now pacing restlessly about his vast study at Karinhalle? Or had his mind become more and more obscured by his injections of morphine?

In Stockholm we felt every day a growing insecurity as we wondered about the German intentions.

Meanwhile I had to deal with some immediate problems. The Swedes, dependent on their foreign trade, have always sailed the seven seas; to be locked in behind the German blockade between Denmark and Norway was like being in prison.

Göring had told us it was impossible to allow our ships to sail from Sweden to America, and my negotiations with Ambassador Ritter in Berlin had led nowhere.

We had tried to persuade the British Admiralty, but without success. We were worried about the British attitude to the problems of economic warfare after the fall of France. We felt that there was a school of thought in London recommending a blockade of the whole European continent, like the blockade applied by Britain when Napoleon was dominating continental Europe. Such a general blockade would have meant that the few remaining neutrals— Sweden, Switzerland and Finland—would have been treated as parts of an economic entity dominated by Germany.

We tried to counteract these tendencies, but one of the British negotiators who came to Sweden, Charles Hambro, told us frankly that the total blockade idea was favoured in many influential quarters in London. The assumption was that the Swedes, surrounded by Germans on every side, had given up their resistance to German pressures. We showed Hambro all our agreements with Germany. He was surprised. He came to the conclusion that 'the concessions made by Sweden were so small that it was incredible'.

Hambro's favourable report helped us, but the British attitude remained rather negative. I lost patience and prohibited the delivery to the British of all statistical information about Sweden's trade. This irritated the British, as they needed the statistics for their planning of the blockade.

Then in November 1940 the British came forward with a positive offer. They would allow four Swedish ships to leave Gothenburg every month and four to enter. This was a success. But there remained the far more difficult task of persuading the Germans.

Hitler, after the occupation of Denmark and Norway, had declared that the whole area round the Baltic should be developed as an economic unit under German leadership. How, from this point of view, could one of the Baltic countries, Sweden, be allowed to carry on its own trade with transatlantic markets, and this with the approval and co-operation of Britain?

I often despaired in my efforts to persuade the Germans, which were doomed to continued failure. When I came back from one frustrating round of talks in Berlin a friend told me the story of the two frogs. Both had fallen into a big pot of milk. One was clear-headed enough to realize the depth of the pot, so he gave up and drowned himself. The other was more stubborn. He trod the milk until it became like cheese. His stubbornness saved him.

In January 1941 I went to Berlin with the firm resolve to achieve a positive result. The Swedish naval attaché wrote in his diary:

I gave a luncheon for the Minister, Gunnar Hagglof, Jacob Wallenberg, Ingemar Hagglof and three German admirals, Schnie-wind, Fricke and Schulte-Mönting. My best wines, including Solera 1847. Rather a success, although I don't know if Gunnar Hagglof's explanation of Sweden's need to carry on shipping to and from the transatlantic markets was a success.

We are so honest. We put our cards on the table . . . The Germans believe that the British must have received something in return for giving their consent. This is a false conclusion, but the Germans don't understand that. 'Nothing for nothing,' they say. I hope nevertheless that this honest discussion will lead to a result.

This was one of many meetings. I had to repeat my arguments a hundred times. At last the resistance of the German Admiralty weakened. In February we signed an agreement on a system for seaborne traffic from Gothenburg to transatlantic countries. Swedish ships were once again able to cross the oceans. In the eyes of the Swedish people, surrounded by German-dominated countries, this access to the open seas was a triumph and a sign of recovered liberty.

But while we travelled between Stockholm and Berlin trying to solve our daily problems with the Germans, the great question of the next German military move still hung over us.

One evening at the beginning of February 1941 Jacob Wallenberg and I were at a dinner in the Hotel Esplanade in Berlin when Jacob whispered that he had something important to tell me. We left the dinner early and walked round the Tiergarten where we could not be overheard.

Jacob told me that his friend Goerdeler had come to the Kaiserhof to tell him in the strictest confidence that Hitler had taken the decision to launch an all-out attack on Russia, probably by the end of May. But how could Goerdeler know this? I asked.

Because, Jacob said, Goerdeler had close contact with Colonel-General Beck, former chief of the General Staff, and Beck had such personal prestige, even after his resignation, that officers of the General Staff called on him to ask his advice.

But, I said, an attack on Russia before the end of the war with Britain would mean a war on two fronts—which was exactly what Hitler had always repeated he would never have.

Jacob answered that Goerdeler's information had always proved to be correct.

On our return to Stockholm we reported this to the Prime Minister and the Foreign Minister. It was, of course, important to try to check Goerdeler's information, and we were soon able to do this. Sweden was dependent on imports of coal from Germany. Already, in February, our ships were having to wait for days, even weeks, in the port of Gdynia, near Danzig, because trains from the coalfields of Upper Silesia were being delayed by important German troop movements in an easterly direction. By the middle of March the railways in Eastern Germany were totally blocked by the eastward movements of troops.

Mr Boheman, the Secretary-General of the Swedish Ministry of Foreign Affairs, informed the British Minister in Stockholm.

At a diplomatic luncheon in March I happened to sit next to the Soviet Minister, Madame Kollontay,* who was a friend. She asked me about my impressions of my last visit to Berlin. I whispered to her that everything I had seen in Berlin indicated that Germany

* Alexandra Kollontay, daughter of a Tsarist admiral. Joined Bolshevik Party as a girl; member of the first Bolshevik Government; Envoy to Sweden, 1932–45.

was preparing herself for an overall attack on the Soviet Union. I saw tears in her eyes as she sat for a moment in silence, then she tapped my hand mildly and said, 'Be quiet, my dear Mr Hagglof. You have no right to tell me this and I have no right to listen to you'. Obviously, Moscow, probably Stalin himself, had given strict orders that the rumours of a German attack should be ignored or denied.

This attitude lent extra credence to an opinion held by many people at that time—that the German troop concentrations were a bluff, intended to put pressure on the Russians so that the Germans could squeeze important concessions out of them. The idea was that Stalin could be scared into giving up vast Russian territories, particularly the Ukraine, rather than fight a war.

I never believed in this theory. Ever since the autumn of 1939 Russia had steadily extended her control over new territories from the Baltic to the Black Sea. We knew very well from our economic negotiations with the Soviet Union that the Russians were rearming as fast as they could. What we had heard about Molotov's visit to Berlin in November 1940 indicated that the Russian Foreign Minister had not been at all in an appeasing mood; on the contrary, he had been very determined and insistent. Quite apart from all this, it seemed to me inconceivable that a people like the Russians would be prepared to give up some of their heartland without a struggle to the bitter end.

During April and May, when nothing could conceal the German troop concentrations in the East, I had many discussions with people in various ministries in Berlin. I found nobody who believed in the theory of extracting concessions from Russia. Everybody expected a massive onslaught on the Soviet Union and they spoke with absolute optimism. In a few months Russia would be crushed in the same way as France a year ago. Then, it was believed, many Russians would rise against the Bolshevik régime.

At a luncheon in June I met a man who told me that he would be leaving his post in Berlin in September to become governor of a province in the Caucasus.

I was surprised by this extreme optimism. In the early 1930s the German Embassy in Moscow and the Ministry of Foreign Affairs in Berlin had been very well informed on the state of affairs in Russia. They had appreciated the strength of the Communist régime, they had always stressed their belief in the strength of the Red Army, and they had watched closely the great progress made in the industrialization of the country. Of course it was not surprising if the Nazi leaders had superficial and often even absurd ideas about Russia. But it was indeed surprising that the military and civilian administration had to such an extent forgotten the teachings of the *Ostschule* of the 1920s and the beginning of the 1930s.

During May and June Berlin became increasingly infected by an almost hysterical excitement; a strange atmosphere, as might precede the launching of a gigantic crusade. Now the fate of Europe was going to be decided.

On the historic date June 22, 1941, when 'Barbarossa', the German master-plan for the attack on Russia, was put into action and 150 divisions crossed the Russian frontiers, the Germans also presented certain demands to Sweden. The principal demand was for permission to send a German division from Norway in transit through Sweden to help the Finns in their fight against Russia. This provoked a crisis in the Swedish Government as the Socialists were unwilling to agree. After some days the Prime Minister succeeded in preventing the break-up of the Coalition Government and the German demand was accepted, but at the same time it was declared that no further concessions would be granted.

A few days later a large Finnish delegation arrived. They presented a tremendous list of goods which they asked Sweden to deliver as a token of willingness to support Finland in her new war against Russia. The leader of the delegation was a member of the Finnish Government, Mr Henrik Ramsay, a man of Scottish descent whom I had long known as a reasonable and pleasant person. He was now totally different from his usual self. He presented the Finnish requests in an almost threatening manner. When I gave a detailed reply, accepting some of the Finnish requirements and declining others, he interrupted me saying, 'It is inconceivable that you can sit there counting in tons and crowns when Finland is deciding the future of Scandinavia for perhaps a thousand years'.

The following day the German negotiator Schnurre called on me. He said he had come on behalf of the Finnish delegation. The answer given by me the previous day must be revised. He had spoken to the Swedish Foreign Minister, he said, and his attitude to the whole problem was quite different. I replied that what I had said yesterday was the answer of the Swedish Government.

I mention this incident as an example of the deep differences in Swedish opinion after Finland had joined Germany in attacking Russia.

My old friend Mr Richert, our Minister in Berlin, wrote on June 23 that 'a victorious conclusion of Germany's and Finland's war against Russia is of vital importance to Sweden. We must all agree on this'. This view was shared by most of the Swedish officers. Within the Socialist Party a great majority was of the opposite opinion.

Soon after the attack on Russia the Germans asked the Swedish Government for substantial credits. Mr Schnurre told me (in almost the same words as the Finns had used) that it was essential that Sweden should give 'a token of her willingness' to support Germany in the heroic struggle against the enemy of Europe—Bolshevism. He pointed out that both Denmark and Switzerland had granted credit. He pointed out that Sweden had recently concluded an agreement with the Soviet Union on the basis of a Swedish Government credit of 100 million crowns. After submitting the question to the Minister of Finance I told the German delegates that the Swedish Government was unwilling to grant credits.

Then the Foreign Minister sent for me. I quote an extract from my record:

Günther said that the question of a Government credit to Germany had to be considered from the point of view of our foreign policy. Our relationship with Germany was very delicate. The Germans were annoyed with Sweden for passively watching the great struggle . . . which the Germans considered as a crusade against Bolshevism. What did it matter if we granted Germany credits of a few hundred millions? To keep the Swedish Army mobilized cost much more.

I answered that if we accepted the present demand for a 300 million credit we were likely to have a further demand for 600 million in six months. Günther replied that my arguments were perhaps valid from an economic point of view, but this was a matter of foreign policy. Other rules of arithmetic had to be applied.

I asked for permission to develop my own ideas on our foreign

[164]

policy. It had been right for Sweden to be very cautious in our relations with Germany during the year after the fall of France. But now Hitler was fully engaged against Russia and if he won this war he would be the dictator of Europe. In my opinion Sweden could not then escape total German domination. Our present Government would disappear and our whole political system would be changed and distorted.

Günther remarked with a smile that it almost seemed as if I hoped for a Russian victory. 'Of course,' I replied. Günther laughed and said, 'You are even worse than Wigforss [the Minister of Finance]'.

When I took this attitude I was doubtless influenced by historical considerations. I had been reading Tolstoy's *War and Peace* since childhood. Every now and then I read parts of Albert Sorel's *L'Europe et la Révolution Française*. Who could avoid drawing parallels between Napoleon 1812 and Hitler 1941?

Everybody remembers the proud utterance of William Pitt: 'England has saved herself by her exertions, and will, I trust, save Europe by her example.' This was said in 1805 when Napoleon dominated the European continent. Few remember the order of the day issued by Tsar Alexander I when his armies, pursuing the fleeing French divisions, had reached Vilna: 'The Russian armies have saved not only Russia. They have also saved Europe.'

It was the Russia of Alexander I which stopped Napoleon's triumphant progress. My hope was that Stalin's Russia would stop Hitler's.

I spent most of the autumn of 1941 in Berlin. The whole atmosphere in Germany had changed. Until the attack on Russia one had seen little effect of the war on the ordinary life of the Germans. Now, with such enormous efforts being deployed in the East, all German resources had been mobilized and the daily life of the ordinary citizen had become dark. This was a struggle for life or death.

In this situation there was much and bitter propaganda against Sweden. The Swedes were accused of sitting comfortably in their corner watching Germany's 'heroic struggle'; Sweden had forgotten her 'historic mission' to defend European civilization against Russia. When Germany had won her victory over the Soviet Union Sweden's day of reckoning would come.

In a speech to the German Reichstag on December 11, Hitler made a sharp attack on Sweden, which, according to the report of our Minister in Berlin, 'provoked an almost hysterical storm of cheers'.

How could there be any doubt that the outcome of the German–Russian war would also be decisive for Sweden?

XIII

The Turning Point

Sitting around a green baize-covered table in Berlin in November and December 1941 it was sometimes difficult to concentrate on arguments for or against Swedish credits to Germany. In the newspapers, reports of the battle for Moscow; on the radio, the Russian appeal to the soldiers: 'You must stand fast!'

In my diary I noted day by day the Russian counter-attacks before Moscow, the reconquest of Rostov, the Russian thrusts at Tula and so on. It seemed more and more certain that the Russians were succeeding in establishing a strong, continuous front line. The Germans would have to muster all their strength for the war in the East in 1942.

Then, on the evening of Sunday, December 7, came the news of the Japanese attack on the American fleet in Pearl Harbour. On December 11 Germany declared war on the United States. These events were the really decisive news. In my diary for December 14, I wrote that it was now clear that Germany was going to lose the war. The turning point had been reached.

But I had little time to reflect on the consequences. It was December 19 before we were able to sign the German–Swedish agreements for 1942. I was then granted a fortnight's holiday.

I suppose everybody feels sometimes the need of solitude in order to think through a problem in all its aspects. I prefer to do this when walking in the country or skiing in the mountains. Then I can come home, sit down and try to crystallize my thoughts in writing. This I did in January 1942. I continued writing my notes after the holiday and eventually had them typed out and gave the only copy to my youngest brother on his thirtieth birthday in April.

I will quote a few points, which at least have the virtue, in 1972, of not being influenced by hindsight:

Even if the war began earlier than Hitler wished—as it probably did—he was nevertheless able to give it a quality worthy of his genius for the dramatic. Then, when France had fallen so swiftly in June 1940, he had his great chance to end the war in Europe by an attack on the British Isles. It is clear—and it was already clear then—that the postponement of an invasion attempt must mean a prolongation of the war, which was bound to be dangerous for Germany.

Later, when Hitler decided to attack Russia, this meant that he accepted a war on two fronts, which his earlier policy had aimed to prevent. This could only be justified if the war against Russia was very short. Now when the war in the East is dragging on and the outcome looks at least uncertain, Hitler's future chances seem very gloomy.

Perhaps he will try to establish contact with the Japanese (if they really wish to co-operate in a systematic way with the Germans?). But perhaps Hitler has other ideas for postponing the catastrophe which—so far as one can judge—must overtake a policy whose chances of success have been dependent on the suddenness of the attack and the brevity of the war.

It is often easier to foresee that a certain event will occur than to predict when. In matters of political action it is the timing which is most important.

When I tried, in the spring of 1942, to speculate on the probable future course of the war there seemed to me to be two points of decisive importance:

How long would it take the Americans to put in a hundred divisions with enough training to be employed in an invasion? I had the greatest belief in the American capacity not only for industrial mass production but also for vast organizational improvisation. But it was difficult to believe that what was necessary would be achieved in less than two years.

The second question was: How long could the war in the East go on? During the battle before Moscow the Russians had brought into action crack divisions from Siberia. This suggested that Moscow did not fear a Japanese attack. In that case there were probably many more divisions to come from Siberia. German officers had told me in Berlin that German Intelligence had discovered, to its own surprise, a great number of Russian divisions fighting at the front which, until then, had been quite unknown to them. The same officers reported that the Russians in the course of the autumn had deployed new and very efficient types of tanks and aeroplanes in large numbers. Was it not reasonable, in the circumstances, to count on at least two more years of war in the East?

Thus, if the war was probably going to last at least two more years before—as I believed—Germany's final breakdown, what could and should a country like Sweden do?

The first and obvious duty would be to go on rearming. The Swedish defences had been weak in 1940 (even if they were very much stronger than those of Denmark and Norway) at least partly because of the massive deliveries of arms and munitions we had supplied to Finland during the winter war. By 1942 Sweden had a relatively substantial and well-equipped army and a small but well-trained navy. The Air Force was full of fighting spirit but its material was insufficient. In spite of the German superiority in the air, it was calculated that the Germans would need some twenty divisions for an attack on Sweden.

As the war in the East put a steadily increasing strain on German resources, an attack on Sweden seemed less and less likely.

In these circumstances it seemed to us Swedish negotiators—Erik Boheman, the two brothers Wallenberg and myself—that we had to concentrate on our relations with the Western Powers, Britain and the United States.

During the sixteen months from the fall of France to the entry of the United States into the war, Britain had had good reason to play for time. This also applied to Britain's relations with Sweden.

The British official historian W. N. Medlicott writes:*

Sweden's neutrality was an asset to the Allies which they could not afford to endanger; pressure had to be limited to what was compatible with a strengthening, or maintaining, of her neutral position. It was as a centre of military intelligence that the value of an independent Sweden was, perhaps, most evident; it also enabled secret communications to be maintained for propaganda and intelligence purposes with Britain's friends in occupied territory and in Germany and it gave quick communication with Russia.

Less tangible (but not without weight in British calculations) were the political advantages of a free, democratic oasis in the

* W. N. Medlicott: *The Economic Blockade*, I, 617.

totalitarian desert. Furthermore, the British Government still hoped, in spite of the German victories, to transport from Sweden important supplies of iron, steel and ferrochrome.

Until 1942 Britain had rightly considered Sweden's position to be very precarious. In discussions in London during the spring of 1941 one expert on foreign affairs said, 'I ask myself which is more probable—a German attack on Sweden or the entry of Japan into the war?'

But from the middle of 1942 the British began to feel that Sweden's position was becoming more secure. They therefore started to press for a harsher Swedish attitude towards Germany. When the American war-trade administration was set up during 1942 they took an even stronger attitude.

We had been prepared for this. We had repeatedly asked to start negotiations, but it was only in the autumn of 1942 that the Western Allies were ready to receive the Swedish negotiator, Erik Boheman, the Secretary-General of our Foreign Ministry. Boheman was well known in London. He had negotiated the agreement between Sweden and Britain in the autumn of 1939 and, being an Anglophile, he had kept the British Minister in Stockholm continuously well briefed not only about Sweden but with such information as we were able to collect in Germany and the German-occupied territories.

When the British Ambassador in Moscow, Sir Stafford Cripps, passed through Stockholm on his way to London in June 1941 he told Boheman he was convinced that there would be no war between Germany and Russia. Cripps was certain that Stalin would make every kind of concession in order to avoid a war. Boheman told Cripps of our detailed information about German preparations and the conviction of leading German officials that Russia would be attacked regardless of any concessions. When Boheman even mentioned the approximate date of the attack—June 20–25—Cripps seemed impressed. On his arrival in London he reported all this to the Cabinet and told Mr Churchill that Mr Boheman had given him excellent arguments for believing in the imminent outbreak of a German–Russian war.

When Boheman arrived in London in October he was met with many British demands particularly for a sharp reduction of the transit through Sweden of German soldiers and arms on their way to and from Norway.

He was also received by Mr Churchill both at 10 Downing Street and at Chequers. Churchill thanked Boheman for the advice given to Cripps. This had saved 'dear Stafford' from making a misleading report to the Cabinet and it had confirmed the opinion held by British Intelligence.

Mr Churchill asked Boheman to give him a survey of Sweden's policy during the war. When Boheman said that Sweden's refusal to permit British troops to cross Sweden in order to fight in Finland had saved Britain from a war with Russia, Churchill retorted, 'You may be right, but why should we discuss such a disagreeable subject?'

Boheman continued his survey by describing the efforts made to speed up Swedish rearmament. Churchill then declared, 'I think I understand your attitude and your policy. You must arm and arm and prepare yourself for the worst. Don't give way to German demands more than you absolutely must. But on the other hand, don't be foolhardy. We do not want another victim'. He repeated twice: 'We do not want another victim'.

When Boheman went on to Washington he was confronted with a much harsher climate. President Roosevelt appointed a special committee to handle the question of the United States' relations with Sweden: Mr Dean Acheson, from the State Department; Mr Dexter White, from the Treasury; Mr McCloy, from the Army Department; Mr Forrestal for the Navy; and Mr Bill Donovan from the Intelligence Service. After a fortnight's discussions Boheman reported to Stockholm that he found the American attitude rather negative. 'The reason is not a dislike of Sweden or a disapproval of the policy of the Swedish Government,' he said. 'The root of the matter is simply an opinion, which the most eloquent explanations seem unable to shake, that Sweden is and must be powerless in the face of German pressure. The Americans assume as self-evident that if the Germans allow Swedish ships to leave and to enter Gothenburg this is because the traffic is in the German interest. It would be better for the world and for Sweden if Sweden were to be as impoverished as possible. Then the possibility of Sweden delivering goods to Germany would be diminished.'

Boheman had to explain over and over again that Sweden's independence was intact, that the Swedish Government had been able to say 'No' to Germany several times, and that both Britain and our Scandinavian neighbours had told us repeatedly that they considered our neutrality to be an important asset both for the present and for the future.

Boheman's explanations and his own personality no doubt made a distinct impression on the Americans, but it nevertheless became clear that it would be impossible to conclude an agreement while he was in Washington, and he returned to Stockholm at the beginning of January 1943.

In February a group of representatives of the American Board of Economic Warfare arrived in Stockholm. This Board had a section of forty-five people for the control of Scandinavia—essentially Swedish war trade. My whole department in Stockholm numbered twenty-two. There were two controllers in Washington for each member of my staff!

Fortunately the group which arrived in Stockholm was led by a wise and very cultivated man, Mr Cass Canfield. They devoted several weeks to an intense questioning of all the Swedish negotiators, particularly myself, in something like the manner of a U.S. Congressional committee.

What aroused very sharp suspicions were the German deliveries of arms to Sweden. One of the American experts claimed that this was a sure sign of a secret political agreement with Germany. I explained in detail that it was economically advantageous for the Germans to sell a small part of their immense arms production to get money to buy Swedish goods. But it was only when I proved to them that Germany had sold vast quantities of arms to the Soviet Union before the German attack in June 1941 that the American suspicions evaporated.

The American group having delivered a massive report to Washington, it was at last decided that we should start negotiations with the British and the Americans, and I was to lead the Swedish delegation.

Travelling between Sweden and Britain was somewhat difficult. If there was only one passenger he was usually put in the bomb-rack of a Royal Air Force Mosquito. One was given a life-belt in case the aeroplane should fall into the sea. What always made me laugh was the whistle which was supposed to be used in order to attract the attention of passing ships when swimming in the North Sea!

Our whole delegation to London flew in an aircraft of the Swedish airline. I don't think we realized how dangerous it was to fly across German-occupied Norway in this relatively slow aeroplane. True enough, we flew during the night, and we succeeded in getting through undetected by the Germans.

As we were approaching the coast of Scotland we ran into a violent snowstorm. The pilot struggled for more than an hour in the blinding whiteness around us until at last he managed to spot the lights of the small airfield at Leuchars and made a landing.

We staggered out into the whirling snow. When we got indoors a man immediately handed me a large tumbler filled with whisky. I asked if I might have it with some water. He gave me an astonished look and said, 'But it's good whisky, sir'.

We travelled by train to London and at King's Cross station we were met by Alexis Aminoff, Secretary at our Legation in London, who shouted, 'Do you know that the Germans have capitulated in Tunis!'

The following day we were asked to go to the Foreign Office. In the ambassadors' waiting-room we were met by the American delegation, led by the Ambassador, J. G. Winant, and the British delegation led by Lord Selborne, Minister of Economic Warfare.

Six weeks of intense negotiations followed. The Allied delegations were constantly presenting us with new demands and I soon found myself in a very difficult situation as I couldn't get clear instructions from Stockholm. Marcus Wallenberg and I, who worked together, realized that the Allied demands went far beyond what the Swedish Government had been prepared to accept at the time of our departure from Sweden. But on the other hand we were quite certain that if we returned to Stockholm and spent a month trying to persuade our Government we would then find that the Allies had raised their demands even higher. We therefore decided to send daily telegrams indicating that unless we received instructions to the contrary we would, at the next meeting, accept such-and-such demands or make such-and-such counter-proposals. In this way we proceeded from one article to another in the long draft agreement.

By the middle of June we had telegraphed the full text of the draft agreement and we received a rather curt instruction to return immediately.

This was easier said than done. Our aeroplane had not been able to wait for us. The pilot felt bound to fly back before the summer nights became too light. He was unlucky. The aeroplane was shot down by the Germans.

We were flown from Dundee to the Faeroe Islands in a big Catalina. Exhausted by six weeks of negotiations, I soon fell asleep. Suddenly I was abruptly awakened by machine-gun fire. It was our gunner, a Norwegian giant with a long red beard, who had started firing in order to keep himself awake.

After landing in the Faerocs we had to find a Swedish safe-conduct ship, and when we did I fell gratefully into my bunk. But I felt happy. We had, after all, reached agreement with both the Americans and the British. Now we had a basis for good relations with the Western Allies.

But in Stockholm I soon discovered that nobody shared my happy feelings. On the contrary. Everybody from the Prime Minister downwards was full of criticisms and reproaches. At the first meeting of the Cabinet after my return I made a long report. It was then decided that Sweden—irrespective of any agreement with the Allies —should cancel all the special concessions granted to Germany for transit-traffic to Norway. It was, on the other hand, decided not to accept the draft agreement drawn up during my negotiations in London.

Our little group of negotiators did our best to argue with the Government. In the end the best we could do was to persuade them to postpone a decision.

That was the first step. Then, through July and August, our group went from one Minister to another arguing in favour of the agreement. By the end of August the Government was at last prepared to give its approval. On September 23 the American–British–Swedish Tripartite Agreement was signed in London.

While I was in London in the summer of 1943 I was in contact with the organization which later was called UNRRA—the United Nations Reconstruction and Relief Agency for the occupied countries. The Swedish Government had decided to make every possible effort to help the suffering countries.

When I explained to the head of the organization, Sir Frederick Leith-Ross, that Sweden's primary interest was to make a very substantial contribution to the relief and reconstruction of Denmark, Finland and Norway, he replied that the needs of south-eastern Europe were much greater and his organization could not allow Sweden to concentrate on her neighbours.

I then recommended to the Swedish Government that we set up our own agency. This proposal was accepted and a government bill was presented to Parliament. I was called to explain our plan to the appropriate parliamentary committee. The parliamentarians took a great interest in the proposals. I had almost an hour of intense interrogation. At my side sat Dag Hammarskjöld, the Permanent Under-Secretary in the Ministry of Finance. His task was to explain the budgetary provisions in the bill. When Dag started off I almost immediately lost the thread. On the wings of abstractions he reached such heights that a heavy-footed fellow such as myself was helplessly left behind. When Dag had finished I whispered to him, 'Do you think any of them understood what you said?'

'No,' smiled Dag. 'That was not my intention. You'll see—we won't have any questions.'

He was right. There was a massive silence for a minute. Then the meeting came to an end.

The Swedish relief programme became quite considerable, reaching a total of some two billion crowns. It was in a sense a miniature Marshall Plan three years before the immensely greater American one.

XIV

'Wir Sah'n Zuviel' *

When I was in Berlin during the autumn of 1940 a young architect
came to see me. He was engaged on working out the quantities of
Swedish granite blocks to be ordered by Hitler's chief architect,
Professor Speer.

The architect gave me a detailed specification of the requirements.
I asked him how he could be so precise in his calculations. He
replied, 'We have complete and detailed plans for all this'. I said I
knew they were planning a big new building for the General Staff,
a stadium in Nuremberg and a high-level bridge across the Elbe.
But what more?

The young man took out a paper covered with figures and explained that the projects I had mentioned were only a small part of
a much vaster programme.

In 1940 the Germans loved to talk about the future. Their future.
The Greater Germany's future. One only had to listen.

The architect explained that all the building programmes were
secret. Hitler wanted to surprise the German people after the
victorious ending of the war by launching enormous changes in
various aspects of the leading German cities.

An avenue far larger and longer than the Champs-Élysées would
lead through the centre of Berlin. On both sides of this 'Avenue of
Victory' gigantic palaces would be built in a style which the young
architect called 'Hitlerian'. He meant, presumably, the greyish,
neo-classical style which marked the new palace of the Chancellor
of the Reich.

'But do you really have enough ministries to fill all these enormous
palaces?' I asked.

'But of course,' he replied. 'Berlin will not only be the capital of
Greater Germany but the capital of Europe.'

There were similar plans for great architectural transformations
in Munich, Nuremberg, Linz, etc.

* 'We have seen too much.'

[176]

'Everywhere in the same style?' I asked.

'Yes, certainly,' he replied. 'The Hitlerian style has the mark of National Socialism. In fact, it is the architectural expression of the soul of Nazism.'

In my mind's eye I could see all the German cities dressed up in this monotonous, semi-military architecture and joined together by new, cement-grey autostradas.

The architect added that the same architectural style would be used in 'the German cities outside Germany'. When I asked which they were, he answered that nobody knew as yet—except, of course, the Führer.

I pondered a great deal on this little conversation. I was reading Rauschning's book *Conversations with Hitler* at about the same time. It was, of course, questionable if these conversations were authentic but my friend Karl Georg Pfleiderer assured me that almost everything reported by Rauschning tallied with what he had heard when, before 1934, he had been carrying on discussions in the inner circles of the Nazi Party. There was no doubt, Karl Georg maintained, that Hitler had in mind a Great German empire comprising the Netherlands, parts of Belgium and France, the whole of Czechoslovakia and parts of Poland. The non-German inhabitants would be replaced by German settlers. Karl Georg was furthermore convinced that the remaining parts of France, Spain and even Italy would in fact be transformed into German satellites. The same would be the case with Scandinavia. These satellites would not be allowed to keep their own armies. On the contrary, certain key cities would remain '*in fester deutscher Hand*' (in firm German hands).

By chance, I could bear out this last statement, for during my negotiations with the German Navy I happened to overhear a young German naval officer giving an older colleague his impressions of a visit to Trondheim in Norway. The young officer concluded by saying that he hoped that such an important naval port as Trondheim would never be handed over to a non-German authority. The older officer answered, 'That, of course, is already decided. Trondheim will remain in German hands'.

If the Germans intended to keep Trondheim, it seemed very likely that they would also retain Narvik in northern Norway, Antwerp, the French channel ports and Brest. Amid these gloomy prospects one could have a small glimmer of satisfaction by thinking of such Hitlerian fellow-travellers as Mussolini, Laval and Quisling. They dreamt of sharing the spoils after victory. Instead they would never be more than Hitler's gauleiters in their own countries, within a Europe under total German domination.

A Europe dominated by Germany. Was this the final goal of Hitler's policies? Rauschning's conversations with Hitler seemed to indicate that the Führer had even more far-reaching ambitions.

In my paper written at the beginning of 1942 I said:

This exaggeration of the element of power has its complement in a very pronounced will to dominate other countries and in the end the whole world.

Italian fascism has its universalistic ideology. It has created an empire. They speak of the Mediterranean as their *mare nostrum*. But the universalistic tendencies of fascism have never been able to blossom because of the obvious limitations of its economic and political basis.

In quite another way the inherent universalistic tendencies have been expressed by German Nazism. The unconcealed lust for power, which is the very heart of Hitlerism, has its natural complement in an ambition to dominate the whole world. Hardly any precursor in history has so obviously been striving for world domination as Hitler.

From the windows of my room in the Hotel Kaiserhof, where I spent seemingly endless months during the war, I could see on one side Goebbel's Ministry of Propaganda, and on the other side the new Chancellery, Hitler's Berlin residence. Outside the heavy copper gates of the Chancellery two men belonging to Hitler's bodyguard were on duty day and night. But Hitler was seldom in Berlin during the war. It was only on rare occasions that I saw the gates being opened and cars rolling into the vast courtyard.

Looking out from my room I often sighed and thought of the Berlin I had known as a young student. Life then had been seething. We young people used to stroll up and down Unter den Linden, chatting and looking for friends. In the theatres new and exciting plays were produced. At the University one could listen every day to lectures of importance.

Now everything was changed. When I dropped into my dear old University I couldn't find a single lecture of interest—except, perhaps, for a study of Nazism. In the theatres nothing of consequence was played. The people in the streets seemed more and more reserved and grey. The only ones with a bit of life were the Nazi bigwigs in their brown or black uniforms. Berlin had lost all spontaneous life. It was now filled only with one man's immeasurable lust for power. How was it possible that people could have changed so totally in a few years?

There were, of course, always some foreign observers who maintained that the German people had not changed in any essential way; that they had always been hard, power-seeking and domineering. This, such people explained, was the German character.

I was never much impressed by this argument. There were obviously a great many Germans who manifested a most detestable brutality and ruthlessness. It was certainly true that the Nazis systematically trained their members, particularly the young people, to be hard and merciless. But anybody who had read history must find it difficult to accept the theory of a hardness and brutality inherent in the character of the German people.

When I was a young student in Berlin in the 1920s I had often listened to discussions of 'the German character'. After the defeat in the First World War and the fall of the Empire, the young Germans were trying to find themselves. I have never found it rewarding to try to define the 'character' of a nation. History has taught me that the 'characters' of nations have changed in the course of the centuries.

Perhaps one could claim that it is easier to describe the 'character' of the French or the British people. Perhaps the difficulty with the Germans may be partly explained by the fact that Germany as a nation-state is a relatively new creation. Another part-explanation may be that Germany is situated at the centre of Europe and that some parts of Germany have for centuries had special contacts with neighbouring countries.

If I had to try to pinpoint a feature of the German 'character' I would mention the German inclination towards the vague and the obscure, to the evasive and the abstruse. Nietzsche has written: *'Wie jeglich Ding sein Gleichnis liebt, so liebt der Deutsche die Wolken*

und alles, was unklar, werdend, dämmernd, feucht und verhängt ist . . .
Der Deutsche selbst ist nicht, er wird, er entwickelt sich.'*

Among my Berlin friends of the 1920s there were many who looked
up to Goethe as their ideal. It pained them, however, that Goethe
had not shown any great appreciation of the German people. In his
famous conversation with Eckermann in 1827 the great man had
declared that many centuries would have to pass before we would
be able to say that it was a long time since the Germans were bar-
barians!

I used to console my friends by saying that Goethe—just as
Nietzsche half a century later—turned against the Germans precisely
because he himself had such a German character. His ambition
during the middle and last part of his life was to reach the high
clarity of Apollo and the Olympic balance of the Ancients. This he
had found in classical Italy. He told Eckermann that only in Rome
had he felt what it is to be a human being. 'To these lofty heights,
to this happiness in my emotions, I have never afterwards been able
to lift myself.'

But in this perpetual endeavour to reach the clarity and balance of
the Ancients, Goethe had to struggle with his own German character, because the German 'character' is rather the opposite of
Goethe's classical ideal.

Hölderlin says somewhere that the soul of the Germans finds its
full expression only in music. But music creates its own closed
world, in which we can exist without being confronted with the
harsh realities around us. Even when the music of Beethoven is
inspired by the composer's revolutionary enthusiasm, the musical
expression is so far from political realities that its effect is only to
inspire a very generalized revolutionary enthusiasm. This is why the
Nazis could shamelessly make use of the liberty-loving Beethoven
for their purpose; at almost all the great Nazi ceremonies extracts
from Beethoven's symphonies were played.

How Beethoven could be used for quite opposite political ends is
shown in a striking way by the first movement of the magnificent

* As everything loves its symbol, so the German loves the clouds and all that
is obscure, evolving, crepuscular, damp and shrouded . . . The German himself
does not *exist*: he is *becoming*, he is 'developing himself'. Nietzsche: *Beyond
Good and Evil*, authorized English translation by Helen Zimmern.

Fifth Symphony. It is a well-known tradition that Beethoven himself said that the opening four notes were inspired by the motto 'Thus Fate Knocks at the Door'. It was probably for this reason that the German radio never tired of repeating this movement, when Germany attacked Russia in June 1941.

But there were some ingenious people in Britain who remembered, about the same time, that the rhythmic pattern of three dots and one dash represents the letter V in Morse code. V for Victory. Thus the famous four notes were used by the BBC to announce their overseas broadcasts and the signal became a symbol of the coming victory of freedom over tyranny.

If—to quote Hölderlin again—music is the full expression of the German soul, the same cannot be said about the visual arts. Here the plastic forms, harmony of colour and clarity of design are too often absent. Wölfflin, to whom I had listened with enthusiasm at the University of Berlin, declared: 'Nordic beauty is not the beauty of the well-defined or the enclosed. It is the beauty of the limitless and infinite.' It is this dimness—sometimes this depth but more often simply a lack of form—which seems to me to be typically German. If this is right, then one can begin to understand why German spiritual life sometimes can reach such prodigious heights and sometimes fall to the very depths of barbarism.

Thus I sat in my room in the Kaiserhof, pondering on the German character and soon coming upon the next big question. If we assume that the disposition of the Germans is such that they undergo change more easily than most peoples, which factor was it that had made them change, in less than ten years, from the liberalism of the Weimar republic to this terrifying Nazi despotism?

I attempted a written answer there and then, at the beginning of 1942:

It is profitable to be in opposition in states where the present seems poor and shabby in comparison with the past and where millions of people have lost their bearings through war or inflation. In such states the discontented are far more numerous than the contented. The three successful totalitarian movements—Bolshevism, Fascism and Nazism—have all gained their support among the masses by opposing *in toto* the existing order. In such an opposition the most disparate elements can be brought together: shopkeepers who have been ruined by inflation; officers who have been 'axed' for economy and are longing for rearmament; workers who have been hit by the economic crises and are demanding drastic social reforms, and many, many others. Such groups would be useless on their own, but if all the discontented are organized as a political instrument they can become effective. This must be done under a totalitarian leadership, otherwise the whole movement would burst asunder at the very moment when it passes from opposition to a position of power.

But this is only the superficial side, the political technique; the real novelty of the totalitarian movements is that they offer the people not political programmes to be worked out on the lines of the old parliamentary parties, but a political faith and even a political mystique. There is an immense vacuum left in many average citizens' minds by the loss of their traditional religious beliefs. The totalitarian movements have the fixed purpose of filling this vacuum with the political mystique offered by the party and its leaders.

'When in the ancient world people began to despair, Christ came to restore them. Now we see again nations despairing and losing their beliefs in the purpose of life. To us Germans, Hitler has come to give our life its purpose and its style and to give us our place in the Divine order of the world.'

That was the Christmas message from the German Minister of the Church in 1936.

'We salute you, Hitler. We believe in God in Heaven who has sent you, my Führer,' proclaimed Ley, the same Minister, at another Nazi rally. Hitler replied, 'I am with you and you are with me! . . . Now I feel that I have the strength to build the new Reich'.

Here is clearly the root of a deliberate modern mystique—a coming together of the people, praying and longing, and the Leader, the god who will reward them and fulfil their needs.

It is the solidarity, the mystical unification, rallying round the personality of the Leader, which are proclaimed to be the highest moral value.

But behind this idolization of the Leader and of the State another mystery is hidden. The State can hardly be the supreme good. The State is too obviously a means and not the final goal. What the really initiated are striving towards is something more. It is the movement itself, with its collective vitality, action, dynamism.

Trotsky speaks of 'the eternal revolution' as 'the innermost mystery' in the religion of Communism. Mussolini exclaims: 'Fascism has no arsenal of speculative dogma. Every system is an error and every doctrine a prison.' In one of the remarkable mono-logues which Rauschning ascribes to Hitler, it is said: 'When the sublime moments of history are before us all false glitter falls away. It is the great rhythm of life which directs the course of events. I restore to violence its age-old dignity of mother of all order and the origin of everything great.'

The real heart of the matter in the totalitarian movements is not the nation, not the race, not even the state, but power and the worship of power.

During the bitterly cold winters of 1941 and 1942, when I sat many evenings looking at the closed copper gates of the Reich Chancellery, it was difficult to recall to mind the enthusiastic crowds which had filled the whole Wilhelmsplatz to salute the beloved Führer after the liberation of the Rhineland or after the incorporation of Austria. At such times during the 1930s Hitler was without any doubt the most beloved leader the German people had had in modern times. When he spoke to the workers in the Krupp factories in Essen, the enthusiasm of those tens of thousands was overwhelming. The German people saw in Hitler the miracle man who could and would realize the highest ambitions of the nation.

To somebody whose business it was to keep track of German opinion it soon became evident that Hitler's popularity began to sink immediately after the outbreak of the war in September 1939. The German people did not want war, certainly not a war against big powers. When Hitler won his overwhelming victories in France, the feelings of the German people rose perhaps a few degrees, but only because the quick victories were assumed to be the surest way to a rapid peace.

It was only when 150 German divisions launched their massive attacks against Russia that the German people really felt the full impact of the war. By the early autumn the people one met in Berlin wore different expressions in their faces. It was not only anxiety about their sons or their brothers on the Eastern Front. It was not only the stringent restrictions, the increasing lack of goods and the ever-increasing air-raids. It was more an increasing anxiety about the darkening future.

One day in the autumn of 1942 my German opposite number, Dr Walter, and I were walking in pouring rain from one Ministry to another in Berlin when he suddenly burst out: 'Yes, if only we can hold out until the Führer has got his new weapons ready.' Walter had information from many quarters, particularly from his friend, General Fromm, the commander of the home army. Perhaps Walter really had information about some new revolutionary inventions; but his sudden outburst could also be read as a sign that he no longer believed in a German victory except with the aid of miraculous new weapons.

I knew enough of the German character to be aware that Germans find it easier than most other Europeans to hide reality behind obscure, profound-sounding words. How many times I had heard them, when faced with some unhappy event, saying to each other, 'Yes, that is just our German destiny.'

We who had to negotiate with the Germans all through the war asked ourselves many times if there was a real possibility of a *coup* against Hitler. During the 'phoney war' many people in London had toyed with this idea. Jacob Wallenberg, who had many contacts with the so-called German resistance, told me then that in his opinion there was no chance of a *coup* except in the event of a great military reverse.

The war in Russia was not turning out to be at all the triumphal victory which Hitler and the great majority of the German people had imagined. But Goebbels's propaganda had succeeded in persuading them that the war in the East was making progress step by step and that the Russians had suffered such enormous losses that they would not be able to hold out indefinitely.

In the best-informed German military circles there began, during 1942, to be much talk about the impossibility of Germany being able to pursue a war on two fronts for several years. The first Germans to speak to me of a possible, or even probable, German defeat were some diplomats and officers. They were all against Hitler and the Nazi régime and some of them belonged to resistance groups.

Dr Goerdeler and his friends did not hide their intention of organizing a *coup* against Hitler. After two years of war in the East, and with the prospect of continued fighting on two fronts, they were convinced that, if they succeeded in killing Hitler, the Generals would be able to order their troops into action which would over-throw the whole Nazi régime. Much depended on the home army under the command of General Fromm.

Personally I didn't have much belief in the chances of the resist-ance overthrowing the Nazi régime. For one thing, there was much too much talk. How could a well-known public figure like Goerdeler visit General Beck one day and the next day call on a well-known foreigner in the Kaiserhof without the omnipresent Secret Police knowing about it? Perhaps Himmler, the head of the Secret Police, was playing the same game as the Minister of Police under Napoleon who let the opposition continue until the police had uncovered all their ramifications.

Secondly, it seemed to me that all the resistance men be-longed to rather exclusive circles of the German aristocracy or upper class. They had few contacts with the broad masses of the people.

Thirdly, I didn't believe that the Generals had such a hold on their soldiers that they would be able to persuade them to fight against the established state and against the numerous and well-equipped divisions of the SS. I wondered if the Generals didn't overestimate their chances. It had been quite different under the Weimar republic, when the Reichswehr was a small standing army, a force, and indeed a world, of its own. After many years of Nazi rule the immense German Army was a people's army, in which every soldier had taken an oath of allegiance to Hitler.

I was more inclined to believe in a slow but steady weakening of the German people's will-power. When I watched the long queues outside the grocers' shops, the overcrowded underground trains with all the white and drawn human faces, the ruins after the air-raids, when I thought of the nine million soldiers fighting their third or fourth winter campaign, I wondered if the end would not be more likely to come through the German people being completely worn out and weighed down by the course of events.

I was thinking not only of physical but also of spiritual fatigue. In spite of all Goebbels's efforts, what was being offered to the

German people by the radio and the Press was meagre and monotonous. Even the great parades and mass meetings, which in the earlier days of the Nazi régime had a sensational and exciting appeal, now seemed out of place.

One day in the spring of 1942 I met by chance an old fellow-student from my days at the University of Berlin in the 1920s. He had a club-foot and was therefore exempt from military service. We walked together for an hour and he told me that the young generation read very little Nazi literature. He was busy organizing the distribution of parcels of books to the soldiers at the front. What the men asked for was, on the one hand, light reading, but on the other hand they also asked for the classical German literature from Goethe to Hauptmann. Nazi literature was only in demand in the SS divisions.

I often wondered if there were, in fact, millions of Germans who, after nine years of Nazi government, looked upon their rule with disgust and even with loathing. Certainly there were some; that I knew by personal contacts. But were there millions? I could see a little evidence pointing in this direction.

In the Tiergarten the benches had been painted with large yellow letters: 'Not for Jews'. This made it impossible for any decent person to sit down on the benches at all. This was not just my reaction. I very seldom saw anybody sitting down.

German friends told me that quite often the poor people in the suburbs of Berlin helped the Jews to get more food. The wearers of the yellow mark of the Jew were not allowed to shop except during certain hours, and then they were put at the end of the queues. But very often food was passed from hand to hand till it reached the Jews.

Were there not many Germans who had heard from soldiers on leave of the terrifying atrocities committed against the Jews as well as the Poles and Russians? Certainly. And I was convinced that many decent Germans shrank in horror from such heinous crimes against humanity.

I happened one day to read a poem which moved me deeply. For a long time I carried it with me. After a walk through the streets of Berlin during the long, dark winters I felt a need to read the poem again. Often I read it with tears in my eyes.

Wir Sah'n Zuviel

Wir sah'n zuviel. Wir sind zu schwer beladen
mit Lastern, Lügen, Wahn und Grausamkeit
mit allen Schrecken dieser wilden Zeit
was sollen wir an friedlichen Gestaden.

Wir wissen schon zuviel von Tod und Grauen,
nun fürchten wir uns vor den hellen Strassen
Wir lebten unter Schatten, wir vergassen
was Liebe heisst und Lächeln und Vertrauen.

Rührt uns nicht an! Lasst uns vorubergehen!
Vergesst dass wir vor langen, langen Jahren
Lebendige und Eure Freunde waren!

Wir haben zuviel Last mit uns gebracht;
ihr würdet unsre Sprache nich verstehen
*denn euch gehört der Tag und uns die Nacht.**

* We have seen too much. We are loaded down too
heavily with torture, lies and insane
cruelty, with all the terrors of those
horrifying years. What are we doing here on
peaceful shores?

We have known too much of gruesomeness and
death, and now we are afraid of
lighted streets. We only lived with shadows,
we forgot what love means, what are smiles
and confidence and trust.

Do not touch us! Just let us pass!
Forget that long, long years
ago we too were alive and were
your friends!

We carried back with us such heavy
burdens; you may not even understand
our tongue, because to you belongs the day,
to us the night.

As a young student I had loved this great, stimulating, puzzling and generous Germany.

It took one generation for Germany to rise after the desolation of the Thirty Years War.

After the defeat in the First World War Germany was able to recover its strength in six or seven years.

How long would it take this time?

XV

Never More Berlin

After my negotiations in London in the summer of 1943 it was
necessary to negotiate with the Germans as we had to modify our
Swedish–German trade in accordance with the stipulations in our
agreement with Britain and the United States. Furthermore, we had
to secure essential supplies from Germany in 1944, and as I expected
Germany to collapse in the autumn of 1944 I intended to ask for
massive deliveries before the middle of the year.

The negotiations were, as usual, heavy and long-drawn-out. For
weeks we sat around the green table in my room in the Swedish
Ministry of Foreign Affairs.

There was one strange interlude in that period. I had a telephone
call one morning from my old friend Karl Georg Pfleiderer, who was
now a Counsellor at the German Legation in Stockholm. He said
he wanted to see me urgently. I asked him to luncheon at my club
the same day. When I arrived he was already waiting. He had brought
a friend whom he introduced to me as Adam von Trott zu Solz. He
was a tall, lanky man with serious and piercing eyes. I thought I
had already heard his name in connection with one of the resistance
groups. I didn't have to wait long for confirmation. Karl Georg
plunged immediately into deep water. He asked me how I had found
opinion in England on the subject of Germany. Before I had time
to reply von Trott began to speak about England with great insight
and sympathy. He had been a Rhodes Scholar at Oxford.

When we had warmed to our subject von Trott told me without
beating about the bush that he was active in the resistance against
Hitler. Germany had already lost the war, he said. It was necessary
to get rid of Hitler urgently. But before the resistance killed him they
would like to know if the coming anti-Nazi German Government
could hope to obtain a reasonable peace. Would the Western Powers
be prepared to offer such peace terms? Had I any information as to
the British and American views on the subject?

Looking into the deep, tragic eyes of von Trott I felt a pang, for

I was bound to tell him that after the adoption of the principle of 'unconditional surrender' by Roosevelt and Churchill at the Casablanca conference in January there was little hope that the Americans or the British would be prepared to make peace with a new German Government except after a total capitulation.

Von Trott thought this attitude both doctrinaire and politically unwise. English statesmen used to be more pragmatic, he said. He supposed that it was Roosevelt who had pressed this hard line.

This was the only time I met von Trott.*

I went straight from the luncheon to our meeting at the Foreign Ministry. The leader of the German delegation made a long summing-up and concluded that he must refuse to accept the Swedish 'dictate'. We must continue our negotiations in Berlin.

When our aeroplane had left Stockholm we were told that a heavy bombing raid was going on over Berlin. We had to spend a day and a night at Malmoe in southern Sweden.

We were met on arrival in Berlin the following day by representatives of our Legation, and their appearance shocked us. There they stood in torn and stained clothes. They told us that the Swedish Legation had been burnt, the Kaiserhof Hotel had been totally destroyed and the German Foreign Ministry, where our meetings were to have taken place, was badly damaged. The Swedish diplomatic personnel, about a hundred people, had already been evacuated to a place near the border of Saxony.

I was driven there to meet my old friend Minister Arvid Richert, who, in spite of everything, seemed as composed and well-dressed as usual. As we talked, walking in the park surrounding the little castle of Altdöbern, we could see in the far distance the red skies over Berlin, which was still partly in flames.

I couldn't stay more than one night in Altdöbern and as soon as a room had been arranged for me at the Adlon Hotel I returned to Berlin.

There was little time for real negotiations. The air-raids went on almost without interruption. In the night it was the British and during the day, the Americans

In the Ministry of Foreign Affairs the German officials tried to adopt the attitude of brave soldiers at the front. But it is probably

* Von Trott was condemned to death by a 'people's tribunal' after the attempt on Hitler's life in the summer of 1944.

easier to be brave in the face of the enemy than when sitting at a shaky table under rattling chandeliers. The old drawing-rooms of Bismarck's day had not been built for bombing raids.

The Adlon had two air-raid shelters. I was told that the deeper and safer was reserved for high Nazi dignitaries. I never saw it. My shelter was used by the ordinary guests of the hotel and the staff. There we sat hour after hour, with little conversation. There wasn't much one could discuss. Everybody knew that the shelters were equipped with devices for listening in by the police.

On my last night in Berlin the British bombers were very late in leaving. The whole of the Adlon was trembling under the impact of bombs falling in the vicinity. I left the shelter and stood for a minute in the monumental entrance hall, now abandoned by all staff. The heavy chandeliers were swinging. The front door had been blown open and I could see a great fire blazing on the opposite side of the Pariserplatz.

I went out of the hotel and walked slowly down the Unter den Linden. The whole broad expanse of the avenue was illuminated by sky-high fires. The hot air blew clouds of dust and paper high above the burning buildings. In the middle of this Dante-esque valley of hell I discovered groups of dark figures. They were prisoners of war, sent out to clear the streets. They cheered the bombs. Round the equestrian statue of Frederik Wilhelm, French prisoners of war danced.

This was my last night in Berlin.

Never more!

XVI

London, 1944

On my return from Berlin and after further negotiations in Stockholm
with the Germans I could report to the Government that we now
had agreements with both the Western Allies and with Germany.

There was general satisfaction. The Prime Minister told me he had
been very reluctant to accept the London agreement of last summer.
'I thought we ought to take one step at a time,' he said. 'If we can-
celled our transit agreements with Germany, that ought to be enough
for some time. But you pressed on and now I see that you were right.
Many thanks.' This was typical of the generous spirit and candour
of Per Albin Hansson.

As a good Swede, he overestimated the solidity of international
agreements. The newly concluded agreements had not solved all our
problems. In January 1944 our Minister in Washington reported a
great deal of irritation against Sweden. The Government in Stockholm thought that it would be better not to wait for a real outburst
from the American side but to begin new talks at once, and for this
purpose I was sent to London.

As it was expected that the talks would take some considerable
time I was given the post of Minister accredited to the Belgian and
Netherlands Government in London.

My first contracts were with the same men who had negotiated
with me the previous summer—Lord Selborne, his closest colla-
borator, Dingle Foot, the American Ambassador Winant and the
head of the Political Department of the Foreign Office, Sir Orme
Sargent. I found that the attitude of all of them towards Sweden
was friendly. Dingle Foot declared that Sweden had gone farther
than any other neutral country to meet the demands of the Allies.
When, by chance, I met Anthony Eden at a luncheon he said that
there had been times when he had worried about Sweden. 'But,' he
added, 'you have managed to muddle through fairly well. I don't
know exactly how you've done it, but now we all have the impression that Sweden can look forward to the coming peace with some
confidence.'

Such criticism of Sweden as there was originated, as a rule, in circles around the governments-in-exile. In my stay in London of more than a year I was faced with only two incidents.

The first was at a supper party given by a Dutch diplomat. Somebody who didn't know who I was began to speak about Sweden's policies during the war. A Dane with his eyes fixed on me, declared, 'After the war there will be good reason to scrutinize all the documents on Sweden's negotiations with Germany and shed some light on those transactions'. I replied immediately that Sweden would be happy to put all the documents on the table. If sometimes we had been obliged to make a few concessions this had been a consequence of the precarious position in which we had been placed after the German occupation of Denmark and Norway. 'And,' I added, 'if Denmark had had a slightly less rudimentary military organization —had it, for instance, been able to defend the Danish airfields for one or two days—then the whole German attack would probably not have taken place.'

The other incident was of more consequence. A Czech diplomat whom I had known in Geneva asked me to a reception in honour of President Benes. My host insisted that Benes had said he remembered me well from Geneva. This seemed rather unlikely as I had been a very insignificant supernumerary on the stage of Geneva, where Benes had been for almost twenty years one of the four or five superstars. Anyhow Benes now invoked our 'old acquaintance' in order to read me a sharp lesson.

He criticized Sweden's 'weak and compliant policy' towards Germany. I answered that we had good relations with both London and Washington. Benes interjected, 'And Moscow?'

He spoke about the German division which had passed through Sweden from Norway to fight against the Russians near Leningrad. I replied that the Russian reaction had been very mild. With raised voice and finger Benes said he had just been in Moscow and he knew the situation exactly. Moscow reproached Sweden for not having restrained Finland from attacking Russia. The Russians were not willing to forgive this. The Finland episode could still be fatal to the future of Sweden. I could only reply that Sweden had tried very hard to persuade the Finns to make peace, but this was not easy as Finland was full of German divisions.

Though the British and American attitude to Sweden was in

general decidedly friendly this didn't prevent the two governments from putting increasing pressure on Sweden in the course of the spring of 1944. The Allied military staffs had come to the conclusion that in spite of continuous bombardments German industrial production was far more efficient than they had expected. They therefore decided to concentrate on certain key industries. The factories were to be bombed and at the same time the neutrals were to be forced to stop deliveries of goods important to those industries. Pressure to this end was brought to bear on Spain, Portugal and Switzerland. Sweden, however, having its tripartite agreement with the Allies, was in a stronger legal position. But the military men tried to get round the agreement through diplomatic pressure.

In my reports from London I told my Government that the American and British delegates found that 'our arguments based on the tripartite agreement were uncomfortably strong'. I added, however, that I assumed that 'we shouldn't decline the new Allied demands *a limine*, but rather discuss them in a friendly spirit'.

In this way we carried on our discussions right up to April 1944 when the British Government, in view of the coming invasion, decided to prohibit all telegrams to and from neutral missions in London.

This ban was very welcome to me personally. I had had more than enough of economic warfare. It was easy to see that the Allies, and particularly the Americans, would exert such pressure that our trade would soon be at a complete standstill. Moreover, I wanted to have much more time to meet people in London, to discuss with the exile governments and try to fathom the future shape of things in Europe.

It was my first duty as the newly-appointed Minister to the Netherlands to present my letters of credence to Queen Wilhelmina. I was informed that Her Majesty maintained the same ceremonial protocol in London as she had in The Hague. I was advised to wear uniform and to be accompanied by a suitable staff. The simple truth was that I didn't possess a correct uniform and hadn't been able to have one made in war-time Sweden. Nor had I any staff. So I had to have my old uniform as an attaché embellished with the many multi-coloured ribbons which had fallen on my breast during eighteen years of diplomatic life. I asked a friend of mine at our normal Legation in

London to be a counsellor for a day at my Legation. He had a splendid uniform which could be made even more resplendent by rows of ribbons.

Dressed up in this way we arrived at the Netherlands Embassy in Portman Square. In the middle of the large drawing-room Queen Wilhelmina, in a high-necked black dress, stood upright, surrounded by her whole government. I made a short speech in French. The Queen put on her eye-glasses and produced a paper somewhat faded by age—obviously the same text as she had used for many years. Having read her speech and handed the letters of credence to the deeply-bowing Foreign Minister, the Queen sat down on a sofa and made a gesture to me to sit at her side. Her Prime Minister, Dr Gerbrandy, and the rest of the Government stood in a semicircle behind the sofa. In a loud voice the Queen asked me about the health of the King of Sweden. As I had been received in audience by him just before my departure I was able to give a lively description of his excellent health. The Queen then asked about the health of the Crown Prince and the Crown Princess, a question I could also answer satisfactorily. Thereafter the Queen enquired about the health of each member of the then rather numerous Swedish royal family. I gave them all a clean bill of health, which happily was well justified but it made the twenty-minute conversation somewhat monotonous.

I met Queen Wilhelmina several times after this and she always put the same questions about the health of our royal family. Once she had received satisfactory answers to these questions she was quite willing to discuss and give her opinions about the world situation. She was well-informed on general questions of foreign policies, but naturally her main interest was the news coming through from the occupied Netherlands, where she had good contacts with the rapidly growing resistance movement. (When I was in The Hague only ten days after the liberation one of the editors of the leading newspaper of the resistance took me round and showed me some of their secret meeting places. In every one I found a portrait of the Queen, sometimes together with a portrait of Marx, and once a portrait of Tolstoy!)

The Queen enjoyed exceptional prestige. In a dispatch from London in the spring of 1944 I wrote:

The presence of Queen Wilhelmina in London is undoubtedly

the basis of the authority of the Netherlands government in exile. A member of the Government—a Socialist and known before the war as an anti-monarchist—has told me how much the Government's position was shaken when the Prime Minister, de Geer, suddenly left London to return to the occupied Netherlands. 'Without the presence of the Queen we would never have been able to get over this calamity so rapidly . . .' The Prime Minister Gerbrandy is quite a personality, deeply religious and inclined to use rather original expressions. When I called on him I found him sitting in a small, almost unfurnished hotel room at a table adorned with an old bible and a large Dutch flag.

To digress slightly, but apropos the Netherlands, when I was on a short visit to Stockholm in the spring of 1945 I was told that the King wanted to see me. At the palace I was ushered into a room which I took to be the King's personal study. I waited for about ten minutes, looking at the numerous portraits and photographs. It struck me that all the subjects of the portraits had been dead for at least a quarter of a century.

When the King entered he sat down to his usual work of embroidery. Now eighty-six, he had aged much since I had last seen him eighteen months earlier. He asked me to tell him about the Netherlands and Belgium. When I described the authority and great popularity of Queen Wilhelmina, the old King said, as if speaking to himself, 'Yes, Wilhelmina has always been a clever girl'. He suddenly looked up from his embroidery and discovered a smile on my face. 'Yes,' he said, 'of course you smile. But you must understand that I always see Wilhelmina as a little girl. She was always so clever at her games when she played in the park at Arolsen.'

This must have been some sixty years earlier.

But to return to London in the spring of 1944, it was certainly the Dutch who, in the shadow world of the exile Governments, had the most evident authority. In a dispatch I wrote:

The Netherlands Government are able to plan and decide their future policies to a greater degree than any of the other governments-in-exile. The Belgian Government's position is weaker. The main reason is obviously their relations with King Leopold. When the

members of this government arrived in London in 1940 they were
—as is well known—in open conflict with their King. At the time
British public opinion was also very bitter in its criticism of King
Leopold. Now almost four years later, there is nothing left of this
attitude. On the contrary, one hears many British people speaking
with sympathy of the King.

The Belgian Government have publicly withdrawn earlier declarations and confirmed their fidelity to the King, but this does not mean
that they have ceased to criticize their sovereign. I have in fact been
surprised by the intensity of their critical remarks. It is certain that
this continuous underlining of their conflict with the King has
weakened the Government's position.

The Belgian Ambassador in London, Cartier de Marchienne, considered himself to be independent of the Belgian Government-in-
exile. He always repeated that he had been accredited by the
authority of King Leopold. I used to call on Cartier every now and
then. King Gustaf had told me that he had an interest in the relations between the Belgian Government and King Leopold, to whom
he was very attached, so I tried to get some news of the King from
Cartier. I can't say I ever succeeded.

When I met him he was over seventy. He had been Ambassador
in London for a very long time and was the doyen of the Diplomatic
Corps. He liked to give advice to a young man like me. '*Mon jeune
Excellence*,' he used to say with a smile (I was not yet forty). 'Do
not believe that London is like any other place. As Ambassador here
you must get used to being addressed by your predecessor's name
for at least five years. It was ten years after my arrival before I
heard somebody whispering, "There goes old Cartier". *Alors, mon
jeune ami, j'ai compris que j'étais arrivé.*'

Cartier taught me that a foreigner living in England should never
try to be like an Englishman. Being a shrewd old boy, he tried, on
the contrary, to stress his foreign character. He spoke fluent English
but always managed to insert some French words and expressions.
He dressed like a French *grand seigneur* of the 1890s. I saw him once
at a shooting party dressed up in a way which made his English
friends whisper to each other, 'The dear old boy—he is so foreign'.

English people like foreigners to be distinctly foreign. To be an
Englishman is such a complicated business. One has to be born in

England, preferably for countless generations, and of course to be educated in England from earliest childhood. Even then it is not absolutely certain that one will succeed in acquiring the mysterious and indefinable qualities of an Englishman.

The outstanding personality among the Belgians in London was, of course, the Foreign Minister, Paul-Henri Spaak. When I presented my letters of credence to him in the most informal way he said, 'I have little to do these days. Do come and have a chat any morning'.

I had met Spaak before the war, when he was a very young Foreign Minister. In his youth he had broken with the upper-class circles into which he was born and, with his natural impetuosity, he had landed first in the left wing of the Belgian Socialist Party. But his inborn common sense and his liking for concrete decisions soon led him to the centre of Belgian politics. I had watched him as he sat listening to the Scandinavian and Dutch Foreign Ministers discussing some fine points in the Charter of the League of Nations. He smiled and he kept silent. I didn't think that there was much contact between him and his Socialist colleagues in Scandinavia.

At his desk in the provisional Belgian Foreign Ministry in Eaton Square Spaak always began his conversation by saying that the policy of Belgian neutrality which he had recommended before the war had been a complete mistake. It was possible to explain why this policy had been adopted, but from an objective point of view it had been a failure. Belgium would probably have been attacked and occupied in any case, but the fact remained that it would have been politically wiser to have made an alliance with France and Britain before the war.

After these introductory remarks, Spaak used to turn to his central idea: the necessity of building an integrated Western Europe. This ought to be the great new mission of Britain. 'What a unique chance the British have. Their first empire fell to pieces in the eighteenth century when they lost the American colonies. Then they succeeded in building up a second, global empire. After the end of this war their colonial empire will in all probability disappear. They have their third chance—to take the lead in creating a new and co-ordinated Western Europe.'

I heard similar ideas from the Netherlands Foreign Minister, the distinguished Dr van Kleffens. The war, he said, had taught the Dutch people that their traditional policy of neutrality was finished. The problem was to find security within a larger grouping of states. He had been studying the possibility of an Atlantic pact, but it was doubtful if the United States would be willing to give any solid guarantees. What he was now aiming at was the formation of an integrated group including Britain, France and the Benelux countries.

One day during the spring of 1944 van Kleffens and Spaak were both received by Winston Churchill. They had long prepared themselves for this meeting. When I saw them the following day they didn't conceal their disappointment. The great man had, as usual, received them with the utmost courtesy. He had listened to them with the closest attention. He had expressed his warm sympathy for West European co-operation. But he had then started to speak of Britain as one of the three World Powers, of Britain as the centre of an empire and of Britain's special relationship with the United States.

Spaak declared that Churchill 'had received his international education in the period before the First World War when foreign policy consisted of secret transactions between the great powers'. With a certain amount of heat, Spaak exclaimed that 'the English refuse to understand that they now have a chance which may not come again in a hundred years—the chance to take the lead in Europe, which in spite of all the destruction of the war offers greater political resources than any other continent'.

Next day I met at luncheon the old French politician Louis Marin, who had just succeeded in getting out of France. Sitting in a small restaurant in Edgware Road he declared with magnificent gestures, 'British policy has to make a choice. One alternative is to play the role of one of the three World Powers. But then Britain will be the smallest of them. The other alternative is to give up competing with Russia and the United States, and instead take the lead in Western Europe. Is it not typical of the English that they refuse to make their choice and prefer to live *dans une équivoque*?'

At the same luncheon Louis Marin told a story about the French police. A French gendarme had been sent to interrogate a person

DIPLOMAT

suspected of belonging to the resistance. The gendarme started with the question, 'Well, what is your opinion of the Germans and of M. Laval?' The man answered with perfect calm, 'About the same as yours'. After a moment's hesitation, the policeman burst out, 'But in that case I must arrest you'.

A pleasant side of my life in London was the friendliness of the men of the Foreign Office, especially Sir Orme Sargent. This tall, lanky man, always in a dark suit, was in a sense the very incarnation of the Foreign Office. He was a man absorbed by his work. During the war he could rarely visit his beautiful eighteenth-century house in Bath. He had a small room at the Travellers' Club, where he spent the nights he wasn't working at the Office. He took his meals in Brooks's Club, so within this triangle—the Foreign Office, the Travellers' and Brooks's in St James's—his whole life was contained. But in his office he had access to all the information of the British diplomatic and intelligence services.

Orme Sargent—'Moley' to his friends—had always been a sworn enemy of Chamberlain's appeasement policy. I was told that when Chamberlain came back from the Munich meeting with Hitler and people were massing in Downing Street and Whitehall to cheer him, Orme Sargent and some other officials were standing looking down from the Foreign Office on the exulting crowds. The door of 10 Downing Street opened and the Prime Minister appeared. Then Orme Sargent was overheard murmuring, 'If he says peace with honour I will throw myself into the street'.

Moley Sargent had much personal sympathy with the idea of a West European grouping and with him I discussed the ideas and plans of Spaak and van Kleffens. Sargent had only once been posted abroad, and that was to Paris. It is true that after his two years abroad he had obtained permission to remain permanently in London, but he often spoke of his liking for France.

We had some long luncheons together at Brooks's when he would discuss British foreign policy as it appeared in June 1944. I quote some extracts from a dispatch I wrote at the time:

It is fairly obvious that the first reason for the British reluctance to be involved in a West European grouping is the fear of disturbing the existing delicate relationship with the U.S.A. It is now more than ever the basic principle in Whitehall to think first of the possible reactions in Washington. Lord Balfour's declaration that 'The English-speaking peoples must always stand together' has, in Winston Churchill's words, 'stood the test of time'. In spite of a great deal of irritation over the capriciousness of American policy-making, the British are deeply conscious of the fact that without the U.S.A. Britain could never defeat Germany nor in the future be able to hold a balance with Russia. The British know, moreover, that they will continue to be heavily dependent on America, not only for the settlement of Lend-Lease but also for the whole future economic policy.

A British friend (Sargent) pointed out that at the time of the Atlantic declaration the British and the Americans found it easy to agree on far-reaching programmes for the future while they were only beginning to tackle the then most urgent practical problems. Today the situation has been reversed. British and American military staffs and civilian administrations are busy handling practical problems in the fullest co-operation while little is done to clarify the great problems of the future. This observation seems to me very relevant.

Well-informed British circles are now rather sceptical as to the possibility of obtaining permanent guarantees for really efficient American co-operation in a future peace organization. Mr Stettinius's visit did nothing to mitigate this scepticism. The British seem to hope for no more than a declaration of principle regarding the maintenance of peace and a promise of military support after an examination of each specific case.

There are of course many pessimists who predict that the Americans will not accept even such a thin declaration. They fear that the world will again be faced with a setback like the Wilson tragedy after the last war. But until further orders British foreign policy is built on the principle: 'U.S.A. first'. The British are convinced that without the closest co-operation with the United States it would be very difficult, perhaps impossible, to secure the future of the Commonwealth, particularly Australia and New Zealand, to reconstruct Western Europe and to establish a positive relationship with Russia.

It is perhaps this last consideration which in the long run will prove the most important. The Russians have a great gift for playing one against another. Many experienced Englishmen believe that the

first condition for a positive relationship with Russia is close British–
American co-operation. It is a new version of Canning's thesis: 'The
New World redresses the balance of the old.'

Lastly, an observation regarding a future peace organization. It is
evident that the spokesmen of the three Great Powers are at pains to
point out that what they now plan is something quite different from
the old League of Nations. 'This time power and representation will
be combined in an entirely different way; this time we will avoid
paying too much attention to the formal sovereignty of the individual
state', etc. It is striking, however, that every time they try to come
down to more precise formulas they fall back on phrases reminiscent
of the Covenant of the League. The 'tentative blueprint' elaborated
by the committee of the American Congress contains hardly anything to surprise an old hand from Geneva. It is easy to quote: *'Plus
ça change, plus c'est la même chose.'* It is perhaps more to the point to
note that it seems to be in the nature of things that every peace
organization which does not take the form of a superstate will meet
essentially the same problems which were discussed over and over
again during twenty years of Geneva debates.

XVII
Approaching the End

It seemed to me in 1944 that some American newspapers were misrepresenting Sweden's war-time policies. I complained about this to Professor Bruce Hopper of Harvard, who had spent some time in Stockholm during the war and was now living in London to work with the American Air Force in Europe as their historian.

He proposed that we should write an article together for the American journal *Foreign Affairs*. I wrote a rough manuscript and Bruce transformed my heavy-footed English into peppery and colourful American. He offered the article to his friend Hamilton Fish, one of the editors of the magazine, who accepted it, and it was published the following month.

In the hospitable home of the Hoppers I met many of the commanders of the American Air Force such as General Spaatz, his Chief of Staff, General Curtis, and the young General Fred Anderson. They were all impressive men, but especially Anderson, who in spite of his youth enjoyed great prestige. Hopper used to say, 'Fred was born to be Eisenhower's successor'.

The night before the invasion of Normandy I was with a group of young Americans. The tension was almost unbearable. When the first news came in the course of June 6 I had the impression that the landings had not succeeded according to plan. It was only in the evening that I got hold of one of my American friends and he assured me that the landings had been 'exceptionally successful'.

Soon afterwards I was called to a meeting with my American and British opposite numbers in the tripartite committee. They appealed to me to stop all Swedish exports to Germany. Fred Anderson told me that General Eisenhower personally insisted on a total stoppage. In the opinion of the Allied military staffs, Germany would break down in a few months.

I was packed off in a Mosquito which made the journey from Scotland to Stockholm in exactly two hours—a record. I didn't feel entirely happy about my mission. It was, after all, I who had signed an agreement with Germany covering the whole year of 1944. Now I was involved in an attempt to stop the exchange of goods foreseen in the agreement.

But there is an old, and perhaps in a way immoral, principle underlying all foreign policy and expressed in the words *'Rebus sic stantibus'*. Who could deny that the situation had changed?

The result of my visit was that Swedish ships ceased to sail to German ports.

I returned to London and on August 25 the liberation of Paris was celebrated. On September 3 the Belgian Government celebrated the liberation of Brussels. The Belgian Minister of Finance, Mr Gutt, told me that he wished me to come to Brussels soon in order to conclude our discussions about Swedish deliveries to Belgium. He would advise me when I should come. It was October when I was given a seat in a military aeroplane for Brussels. The first enthusiasm after the liberation had already evaporated. The life of the ordinary Belgian was dominated by the lack of goods, unemployment and rapidly mounting inflation. The most disquieting problem for the Government, however, was their relations with the various resistance groups, some of which threatened to march on Brussels. It was only after the intervention of the British commanding officer, General Erskine, and after tense negotiations with the Government that the resistance groups finally agreed to lay down their arms.

I spent the next several weeks discussing Swedish deliveries of goods for Belgian reconstruction. Just as I was about to leave for London, Brussels was shaken by the news of the sudden German offensive on December 16 when von Rundstedt's divisions broke through the American First Army's lines near Bastogne and Stavelot. Brussels was like a maelstrom. It seemed as if all the troops under General Montgomery's command had to pass through the capital on their way to the front. I sat waiting for three days to get an aeroplane. When at last we took off we were hindered by fog and were obliged to land at Exeter.

This was a difficult time for travelling. I had to go back to Sweden to get the Government's approval of my agreement with the Belgians. My American friends in London asked me why I always flew in Mosquito planes; the American Air Force now had a big airfield in Norfolk specially for flights to Northern Europe.

When I arrived in Norfolk I certainly found an impressive airfield with vast barracks and several hundred men, but unhappily for me no aeroplane had so far left for Scandinavia. I had to wait for more than two weeks. It was a strange experience suddenly to be living in surroundings as American as Idaho or Missouri. There seemed to be no contact whatever between the American base and the surrounding countryside. Most of the American servicemen had never bothered to make the twenty-minute bus journey to see the beautiful and utterly English city of Norwich.

We had gradually become a group of four waiting for a flight to Stockholm—three American diplomats and myself. One day we were told that we were due to fly that evening. We found an old Dakota waiting for us. The pilot explained that there was no heating, so we were dressed up as Arctic explorers. Eventually we were handed two bottles of whisky and advised to take a swig every half-hour.

In spite of the fur coats and the whisky, it turned out to be a freezingly cold flight. After eight hours the aeroplane landed. We stumbled out, only to find ourselves on the same old airfield in Norfolk. The pilot, after some hesitation, had decided that the risks in flying across central Norway were too great.

After three more days of waiting we took off again. This time we sat shivering in the aeroplane for twelve hours. The pilot had chosen his route round the North Cape. When we landed in Stockholm I felt ill. The whisky hadn't been efficient enough. I had to stay in bed for more than a fortnight.

When my Belgian agreement had been approved I returned to London, but only for a few days. Fred Anderson invited me, together with General Curtis and Bruce Hopper, to visit the Allied headquarters in France. We stayed in a small château not far from Versailles. There were more Generals than I had ever seen before.

Paris, seven months after the liberation, made a very depressing impression on me. There was a flourishing black market where one could buy anything with dollars, pounds or Swedish crowns. But outside the black market the lack of goods was increasing, and so were the prices in francs. The great majority of the French people must have been half-starving.

Three times during my short stay in Paris stones were thrown at the car in which I was travelling, an American military car flying the flag of a General. In the officers' mess the talk was lively. Most of the American officers seemed to dislike France and the French. The nation they all admired most was without doubt Russia. It was the Russians who had made the greatest war effort. It was with their help that the peace was going to be made. When Bruce Hopper made a critical remark about the lack of freedom of the Press in Russia he was ticked off rather rudely. He whispered to me that he wouldn't argue. 'They will soon know better,' he said.

From Paris we flew to Stockholm to clear up some questions regarding the many American pilots who had landed in Sweden after bombing raids on Germany. Fred Anderson ordered our pilot to fly straight across German-occupied Denmark. Six fighter planes from American airfields in West Germany came to escort us. It was a brilliantly sunny day at the end of March. From the air I could now look down on Germany, the Nazi Germany which was now at its last gasp.

A few days later I was in Brussels to sign the agreement. It was a pleasure to have for once conducted negotiations without any dissensions and to sign an agreement in which Sweden was the 'giving' partner.

The Finance Minister Gutt was very eloquent: 'The Goddess of Peace will bring us all many gifts. But Sweden has hastened to bring us her gifts already, before the peace. This we will not forget.'*

* I had, of course, assumed that this agreement, like almost all other agreements, would soon be forgotten. It was a pleasant surprise to receive, on the twenty-fifth anniversary, a letter of remembrance and thanks from the then Belgian Minister of Commerce.

XVIII
V.E. Day

April 1945 was not a time for everyday work. I sat in my house in Brussels for hours listening to the BBC.

At the beginning of the month Canadian troops were fighting close to Belgium's northern frontier with the object of liberating Holland. The British and Americans were encircling large German army groups in the Ruhr area. The Russians had conquered Hungary and on April 13 entered Vienna.

The previous day the news of the death of President Roosevelt had been announced. All over the free world there was a wave of sorrow. I must confess that I cried. Earlier than any other leading Western statesman Roosevelt had foreseen the enormous threat which Hitler and his Nazi state represented to the whole civilized world. With great political courage and considerable cunning he had carried through Congress his plan for 'Lend and Lease', which brought immeasurable help to Britain. As soon as the United States came into the war Roosevelt gave first priority to Europe in the face of claims put forward by powerful groups in favour of the immediate deployment of the main American forces in the Pacific. Where would we Europeans have been without Roosevelt?

On April 28 Mussolini was murdered near the Swiss frontier and two days later Hitler committed suicide in his Berlin bunker.

After the German capitulation on May 7 it was proclaimed that the following day should be celebrated as European Victory Day—'V.E. Day'.

All the Allied embassies in Brussels sent out invitations to celebration parties and several Belgian friends organized private parties. When I was dressing that morning I suddenly realized that I didn't want to go to these victory celebrations. Certainly I was as happy as anybody else that the victory had been won. But I felt very deeply that I hadn't made the slightest contribution to this victory. Sweden had been neutral and I had assiduously served my country's policy.

I would willingly have celebrated Sweden's escape from the war, but to appear as a neutral guest in the company of the people who had really fought against Hitler and his hordes—this I could not bring myself to do.

To escape from the saddening thoughts which led me to this conclusion I had sought consolation during the night in my beloved *La Chartreuse de Parme*. For perhaps the thirtieth time I read the immortal description of the young Fabrice del Dongo at the battle of Waterloo. It suddenly occurred to me that I could take a bus from Brussels southwards to Waterloo, Mont St Jean and La Belle Alliance. Waterloo is only eighteen kilometres from Brussels. The bus continued on its way, passing Mont St Jean, where Wellington had such a strong defensive position, and stopping at Plancenoit, where Lobau fought his brave rearguard action to save Napoleon's armies from total destruction.

It was a brilliant early summer's day. I walked the country lanes from one village to another, and by midday I had returned on foot to Waterloo, but there I found crowds assembling and military bands playing.

I turned instead to the beautiful Fôret de Soigne and in the shade of impressive oaks I found a peaceful little inn. There I sat, a lone neutral with a glass of Belgian beer.

My thoughts turned naturally to Sweden. How were the Swedes celebrating the Allied victory? Surely the Prime Minister would speak to the people. Surely he would speak of the Swedish Government's firm foreign policy which had been Sweden's salvation from the war. This would probably be the slogan for the future. The Swedish people would have their traditional belief in neutrality confirmed, for once again the pursuit of neutrality had succeeded for them.

During my last visit to Sweden I had heard most people speaking in this vein. Only the former and future Foreign Minister Unden had declared that the lesson of our experiences during the war was that neutrality is 'a frail protection'.

Sitting at my table in La Fôret de Soigne I repeated these words. At the outbreak of the war twenty European states declared themselves neutral. Three of the neutrals were annexed to the Soviet Union—Estonia, Latvia and Lithuania. Eleven were attacked and most of them occupied—Denmark, Norway, the Netherlands,

Belgium, Luxembourg, Finland, Romania, Hungary, Yugoslavia, Bulgaria and Greece. Only six of the twenty were spared to pursue their policy of neutrality—Sweden, Switzerland, Turkey, Spain, Portugal and Ireland.

These are statistics which would make even the most optimistic insurance man hesitate.

But—many Swedes persist in saying—Sweden succeeded in saving herself from the war. This is a fact. Why should we Swedes have doubts about neutrality?

I remembered the Dutch political leaders in the 1930s. With the greatest self-confidence they brushed aside all doubts of the strength of neutrality with a reference to the fact that the Netherlands had succeeded in coming intact through the First World War. 'This is an inescapable fact,' the impressive Prime Minister Colijn told me after an equally impressive luncheon at the Hotel des Indes in The Hague.

Today, six years later, the Dutch political leaders were of exactly the opposite opinion, thanks to the 'inescapable fact' of having been attacked and occupied.

In discussions with friends in Sweden I had encountered, on this point, the remark that what had happened showed that such countries as Sweden and Switzerland were so placed geographically that they formed a much better basis for neutrality than Finland, Denmark, Belgium or Holland.

Thus it is necessary to examine the reasons why Sweden was not attacked during the Second World War. Hitler attacked and occupied Denmark and Norway because he wanted to prevent an Allied intervention in northern Scandinavia and at the same time gain control of the Norwegian coast. To achieve these aims Hitler didn't need to attack Sweden. But if his daring attack on Narvik had failed, and the Western Allies had seized northern Norway, Sweden would have been in an extremely dangerous situation, with the strong probability of a German attack before or after the decisive battles in France.

Throughout the spring of 1941 it was, in my opinion, necessary to assume the possibility of a German invasion of Sweden in order to secure Germany's northern flank before the great attack on Russia. Hitler made war on Yugoslavia and Greece in order to secure himself against possible British landings on his southern flank. Why not also on the northern flank?

Later in the war Churchill often toyed with the idea of Allied landings in northern Norway. His Chiefs of Staff had great difficulty in restraining him. The thoughts of Churchill and Hitler at this point were strikingly alike. The Führer was often deeply worried about the possibility of British landings in the north. If Churchill had not been dissuaded by his Chiefs of Staff Sweden's position would again have become critical.

One could continue this analysis of Sweden's position during the war. What is essential is to admit that of the many factors contributing to the result that Sweden was *not* attacked, only a few were under Sweden's own control.

One of my friends in Stockholm exclaimed with obvious alarm, 'But you don't mean you would like Sweden to abandon her policy of neutrality after the war?'

Abandon it for what? What alternatives would Sweden have after the war? No, what I considered essential was that we should realize that the experiences of the war had proved that neutrality is 'a frail protection'. It was essential that we should refrain from creating a myth that Sweden—thanks to 'an able and firm foreign policy'—had escaped the fate of our Scandinavian, Belgian and Dutch neighbours.

It had become fairly certain—at least in my opinion—that the United Nations Organization, as planned at the Dumbarton Oaks conference, would in many ways resemble the old League of Nations. Churchill had declared that the new organization conformed to the spirit and principles of the old Covenant, but he had added, 'The new organization has been invested with the necessary authority'. What did this authority consist of? I had listened to the debate on the United Nations Charter in the House of Lords. Lord Cecil of Chelwood, the former Lord Robert Cecil, had touched on the crucial point: 'If it means that the five Great Powers all have to agree, it means that in the ultimate question of the peace of the world any one of the Great Powers can use a veto . . . If one of them should be the aggressor, I am sure that the veto would be used.'

But if, on the one hand, neutrality had proved to be 'a frail protection', and, on the other hand, the new world organization for peace proved almost as brittle as the old League of Nations, where could a state like Sweden find a basis for its future?

It is clear—I said to myself in a loud voice—it is certain that we will have to build a new consolidated Europe. It is certain that the

Soviet Union will not co-operate, not at least until a time in the distant future. But Western and Northern Europe ought to form the first grouping. In due course, the vanquished states would have to join in this European brotherhood.

I was so excited by these thoughts that I started to sing to myself as I walked along the narrow lanes through La Fôret de Soigne.

Sweden must have a positive task in the coming world. We mustn't shut ourselves up in 'a paradise for ourselves'. The future belongs to those who will co-operate in constructing a new, free, strong and open-minded Europe.

Such was my European Victory Day.

Epilogue

It was easy to have visions on the day of victory. The following days and years were to bring disappointments and setbacks.

I was sent to Moscow in 1946. As head of the Swedish Legation I had to settle some questions outstanding between Sweden and Soviet Russia since the war. I was a witness of the breakdown of the war-time alliance between the victorious Great Powers and of the ensuing developments leading to the Cold War.

My Government then sent me to New York as permanent delegate to the United Nations. To somebody who had spent many years at the League of Nations in Geneva it was a fascinating but also a somewhat disappointing experience to compare the new City of Peace with the old.

In 1948 I was appointed Ambassador in London. The following nineteen years were incomparably the happiest of the forty-five years of my diplomatic career.

But that is another story, which I shall tell in due course.

INDEX